Praise for *On Preaching*

Pastor Charles has provided a tremendously practical guide to the entirety of preaching. Whether you have been preaching for 50 years or 5 weeks, you will find it helpful.

> GEORGE E. HURTT
> *Pastor-Teacher, Mt. Sinai Missionary Baptist Church*
> *of Los Angeles*

Timely. Practical. Insightful. Helpful. Refreshing. These are just a few ways I would describe H. B. Charles, Jr.'s new book, *On Preaching*. This book stands uniquely to offer tested wisdom from a voice of experience, integrity, and passion, through a man committed to communicating for God. Your seriousness about the ministry of preaching demands that you take in this book.

> ROMELL WILLIAMS, JR.
> *Senior Pastor, Lilydale Progressive Baptist Church of Chicago*

In an age where the focus on the authority of Scripture and true life-changing expository preaching is deficient in pulpits across America, H. B. Charles, Jr. has used his almost thirty-year pulpit ministry to guide preachers away from the personality of the preacher to the process of effective preaching.

> LANCE A. MANN
> *Senior Pastor, St. Luke Baptist Church, Crocket, Texas*

Uniquely gifted in the pulpit and with pen, my good friend and neighbor H. B. Charles gives us a practical yet profoundly gripping challenge to do the work of an expositor. Pastors everywhere need to read this book, and even more importantly, practice its content.

> MAC BRUNSON
> *Senior Pastor, First Baptist Church of Jacksonville, Florida*

For a number of years I have been challenging African American pastors to put their homiletical preaching brilliance to writing. How delighted I am to see that my ecclesiastical son in the gospel has done exactly that. What we have before us is that which challenges us to go from devotion to delivery, from meditation to message, and from studies to sharing. As a result, I salute my son in this great presentation.

DR. MELVIN WADE, SR.
Senior Pastor, Mt. Moriah Baptist Church of Los Angeles

On Preaching has been written out of the soul of H. B. Charles, Jr. His experience, study, reflection, and conviction may contribute in some measure toward encouraging the preachers who may use it in becoming greater preachers of the Gospel of Jesus Christ.

JOHN A. REED JR.
Senior Pastor, Fairview Baptist Church, Oklahoma City, Oklahoma

I am so glad that H. B. didn't wait any longer to put in print these personal and practical conversations concerning biblical preaching. I feel like I am walking or sitting with H. B. as he reflects not only on the ministry of preaching but on how he has sought to do it as God has enabled him. For those interested in "rightly dividing the word of truth" in the local church, this book is helpful, balanced, encouraging, and honoring to the Lord of the Word and the Word of the Lord. Clarity, humility, and authenticity permeate each concise chapter. I highly recommend it!

DAVID OLFORD
Olford Ministries International

From teen preaching to preeminent pulpiteer, Dr. H. B. Charles, Jr has again demonstrated through pen and paper what he so effectively and efficiently does through his pulpit proclamation, resulting from his prior preparation. Acts 1:1: "*All that Jesus began to do* (example) *and teach*" (explanation).

Read this book ON PREACHING and PRACTICE it with great profit.

A. LOUIS PATTERSON, JR
Mount Corinth Baptist Church, Houston, Texas

H. B. CHARLES, JR.

ON PREACHING

PERSONAL & PASTORAL INSIGHTS FOR THE
PREPARATION & PRACTICE OF PREACHING

MOODY PUBLISHERS

CHICAGO

All Scripture quotations, unless otherwise indicated, are taken from *The Holy Bible, English Standard Version.* Copyright © 2000, 2001 by Crossway Bibles, a division of Good News Publishers. Used by permission. All rights reserved.

All websites listed herein are accurate at the time of publication but may change in the future or cease to exist. The listing of website references and resources does not imply publisher endorsement of the site's contents. Groups and organizations are listed for informational purposes, and listing does not imply publisher endorsement of their activities.

Edited by Christopher Reese
Interior design: Ragont Design
Cover design: Geoffrey Sciacca
Cover image: Wavebreak Media / 123RF
Author photo: Derrick Wilson

Library of Congress Cataloging-in-Publication Data

Charles, H. B.
   On preaching : personal and pastoral insights for the preparation & practice of preaching / H.B. Charles.
      pages cm
   Includes bibliographical references.
   ISBN 978-0-8024-1191-4
   1. Preaching. I. Title.
BV4211.3.C49 2014
251—dc23

                                                      2014001987

We hope you enjoy this book from Moody Publishers. Our goal is to provide high-quality, thought-provoking books and products that connect truth to your real needs and challenges. For more information on other books and products written and produced from a biblical perspective, go to www.moodypublishers. com or write to:

Moody Publishers
820 N. LaSalle Boulevard
Chicago, IL 60610

7 9 10 8

Printed in the United States of America

I joyfully dedicate this book to the beloved members of the Mt. Sinai Missionary Baptist Church of Los Angeles. You introduced me to the Lord Jesus Christ. I preached my first sermon to you, as an eleven-year-old boy. At the age of seventeen, while just a senior in high school, you called me to be your pastor. And you faithfully and eagerly listened to me preach and teach the Word to you for eighteen years. Enjoying some good preaching and enduring a lot of bad preaching, you continually encouraged and supported me. Most of the principles I write about in this book, I learned while serving you. And I practiced them on you! I am what I am because of the investment you made in me.

I thank my God in all my remembrance of you, always in every prayer of mine for you all making my prayer with joy, because of your partnership in the gospel from the first day until now.

PHILIPPIANS 1:3–5

CONTENTS

Part 3: Points of Wisdom for Preaching

Introduction

MY PREACHING CRISIS

I go through a "preaching crisis" every year. I am not sure when in the year it is going to come. But it never fails to happen. I inevitably go through an annual season when I become extremely frustrated with my preaching and determine that I need to work harder to become a better preacher.

For the record, I am never satisfied with my preaching. I know all too well that I have not "arrived." Every now and then, I finish preaching and feel like I hit it out of the park. Most weeks, I am grateful just to get on base—even if I have to lean into a pitch and take one for the team. Like most pastors, I can't stand to hear or see recordings of my preaching. It's cruel and unusual punishment. I try to press on with my regular preaching duties without paying much attention to the weaknesses in my preparation and presentation. But that only works for so long. At some point, I come face-to-face with the fact that I have a long way to go as a preacher.

This preaching crisis, as I call it, is not about my understanding of the Word of God. I readily accept my ongoing need and duty to grow in the grace and knowledge of Jesus Christ (2 Peter 3:18). My father would often say that the Word of God is pregnant with truth. The more you study it, the more it gives birth to new insights into

God's revelation. You can never exhaust the riches of Scripture. We will always be students of the Word, never experts. If you think you have mastered the Scriptures, please get out of the pulpit before you do great harm. We perpetually need to feed on the pure spiritual milk for our nourishment in Christ, just like every other redeemed sinner (1 Peter 2:1–3). The difference is that once we learn the truth and apply it to our lives, our work is not done. We must proclaim it.

The call to preach the Word is the great privilege and awesome responsibility this book addresses. There are times when I have worked hard to get the meaning of the text, but have failed to communicate that message in a clear and compelling manner. I have unintentionally miscommunicated the text because my sermon was sloppy. When I catch this happening in my preaching, I get a renewed determination to be a better preacher.

There are three kinds of preachers: the ones you can listen to, the ones you cannot listen to, and the ones you must listen to. I desire to be the kind of preacher that you must listen to. But that requires more than desire. It requires hard work. And the hard work never ends, if you take your preaching assignment seriously.

The last time I went through my preaching crisis, I responded the way I normally do. I read or reread several books on preaching. I listened to a lot of preaching. And I got feedback from trusted advisors and colleagues. But I did something new. I started writing articles on various aspects of preaching. As one who writes as he learns and learns as he writes, I found this process immensely rewarding. As I wrote, I posted the articles on my blog site and received many positive responses. Of course, not everyone agreed with my homiletical views. But the fact that other preachers found these posts to be thought provoking, challenging, and helpful encouraged me to keep writing. One day I perused the file of articles, and it dawned on me that a book was emerging. Thankfully, my publisher agreed.

This volume is not a textbook on preaching. It is a handbook of best practices, not a technical or theoretical treatise of hermeneutics or homiletics. I hope seminarians will benefit from this book. But it is not intended for students in the classroom. It is meant for preachers in the trenches. It is for the new preacher who is just beginning his pulpit ministry. It is for the seasoned preacher who is trying to sharpen his skills. It is for you, no matter the stage of ministry you are in.

I am not an expert trying to show you the way it is done. I am a fellow traveler hoping to partner with you on the journey. We are in this together. As you encounter concepts in this book you find beneficial, by all means, use them. Where you see things from a different perspective, push back. Think through the material in light of your own context of ministry. My way is not the only way. And it may not be the only way for you. But I pray this book will lead you to a "preaching crisis" that strengthens your resolve to faithfully preach the Word of God and the testimony of Jesus Christ.

Part 1:

PREPARATION
FOR PREACHING

Chapter 1

PREACH THE WORD!

What is preaching?

The term Paul used in 2 Timothy 4:2, where he charges Timothy to preach the Word, was originally a political term, not a religious one. It referred to the function of a herald. If the king had a message to get out, he couldn't just call a press conference and have all the news media publish or broadcast his remarks. He would dispatch his herald to deliver his message to his people. When the herald arrived at a city, he would cry out his message in a grave, formal, and authoritative voice. When he spoke, the people did well to listen and take heed. To ignore the herald's message was to reject the king's authority. And the herald would be careful to proclaim the king's message with clarity and accuracy. To misrepresent the king's message was just as dangerous as rejecting it.

This is the picture that naturally came to Timothy's mind when Paul charged him to be God's herald who faithfully proclaims the Word of God. And the assignment has not changed for those of us who preach today. We must preach the Word.

It is God's will to save the lost and sanctify the church through faithful, biblical, Christ-centered preaching. Unfortunately, biblical preaching is not a high priority for many people looking for a church. Secondary things like music styles, ministry programs, and congregational prominence are often deemed more important than biblical preaching. In some instances, church shoppers consider a congregation's available parking spaces before they ever consider that congregation's doctrinal positions. Consequently, many pastors and churches—seeking either survival on one hand or success on the other—have compromised the centrality of preaching.

But preaching is and has always been the distinguishing mark of the true church of Jesus Christ. Faithful preaching is the essential mark of the true church, because if a church faithfully preaches the Word and allows its life to be shaped by it, everything will eventually fall into its proper place. Conversely, a church's apparent success is only incidental if it does not have a biblical standard of measuring, sustaining, or renewing its ministry. Biblical preaching is the central, primary, and decisive function of those God calls to shepherd the church.

Paul's charge to Timothy is the Lord's charge to every preacher: Preach the Word! This divine command obligates us to preach; moreover, it specifies what we are to preach: the Word. The importance of preaching rests in its content, not in its function. Our preaching is not the reason the Word works. The Word is the reason our preaching works. This is the biblical priority of pastoral ministry. We are charged to carry out a holy function—preaching. And we are charged to herald a holy message—the Word.

But what does it mean to preach the Word?

PREACH THE CONTENT OF THE WORD

The herald was on assignment to deliver the message of the king. It was not his message. And he did not have editorial authority over it. He could not change the message to suit the crowd. Neither can we. The pulpit is not the place for personal testimonies, political speeches, group therapy sessions, motivational talks, self-help advice, worldly philosophies, or scientific theories. The pulpit is the throne of the Word of God. Therefore, the sacred text must be the priority of our preaching.

One noted scholar often says that those who preach should always be pointing to the text. Literally. If you are gesturing with your right hand, you should keep your left hand's finger on the text. If you reverse hands for gesturing, you should also reverse hands for holding your spot in the text. This is a practical way to remember that our preaching should always point to the text. We must preach "the sacred writings" (2 Timothy 3:15). And we must preach "all Scripture" (2 Timothy 3:16). Did you get that? Preach the Bible. But don't just preach your pet topics, hobbyhorses, or favorite doctrines. Preach it all. Strive to end your ministry with the words of Paul: "Therefore I testify to you this day that I am innocent of the blood of all, for I did not shrink from declaring to you the whole counsel of God" (Acts 20:26–27).

PREACH THE MEANING OF THE WORD

We must preach the content of Scripture. But biblical preaching involves more than reading, quoting, or mentioning Scripture in your sermon. The content of our messages must line up with the meaning of the text. Paul wisely counsels, "Do your best to present yourself to God as one approved, a worker who has no need to be ashamed, rightly handling the word of truth" (2 Timothy 2:15).

Scholars are not sure what particular nuance Paul intended when he speaks of "handling the word of truth." But the big idea is clear. The pastor-teacher who is approved by God and needs not be ashamed of his work must have an unwavering commitment to the faithful exposition of the Word of truth. Ultimately, there are only two ways to preach—by exposition or by imposition. Either your preaching explains the God-intended meaning of the text or it sinfully imposes human speculation onto the text.

Think about it. When you go to the airport to catch a flight, you are clear about the destination, flight number, and time of departure. But there is another key piece of information you need before you travel. You may not think about it until you get to the airport. But when you arrive, the gate number becomes all-important. You don't just go to any gate and hop on a plane. You go to the specified gate, because going to the wrong gate, even if it's just the next one over, can lead you far from your intended destination. Likewise, a lack of precision in handling the Scriptures can lead people far away from God, rather than closer to Him.

PREACH THE FOCUS OF THE WORD

When Paul charged Timothy to preach the Word, he specifically had the Old Testament in mind. The writing of the New Testament canon was still in process, even as Paul wrote the words of 2 Timothy. The Old Testament was the collected body of Scripture from which the early church preached. Yet Timothy's preaching of the Old Testament was to be done as a minister of the new covenant (2 Corinthians 3:6). He was to read the Old Testament texts with New Testament eyes. His preaching was to focus on the divine person and redemptive work of Christ.

The Lord Jesus Christ was the focus of Paul's preaching. "We preach Christ crucified," he declared (1 Corinthians 1:23). "For what we proclaim is not ourselves," he testified, "but Jesus Christ as Lord, with ourselves as your servants for Jesus' sake (2 Corinthians 4:5). Paul preached Christ. And when he exhorted his protégé to preach the Word, he clearly intended that the message of Christ should be the focus of his proclamation of Scripture.

On one occasion, someone complained to Charles Spurgeon that all his sermons sounded alike. "And so they should," he replied. "First I take a text, and then I make a beeline for the cross." Likewise, our preaching should unapologetically focus on the virgin birth, impeccable life, substitutionary death, glorious resurrection, and imminent return of Jesus Christ. "Him we proclaim," the apostle boldly declares, "warning everyone and teaching everyone with all wisdom, that we may present everyone mature in Christ" (Colossians 1:28). It is not Christian preaching if the person and work of Christ is not the centerpiece of the message. We are to be heralds of the Word and witnesses for the Lord Jesus Christ.

What are you preaching?

Chapter 2

THEOLOGICAL TRAINING

As a boy preacher, my father let me preach one Youth Sunday at our church. After the service, a brother commended my sermon, concluding, "Junior, in a minute you are going to out-preach your old man." When I later told my dad about the statement, I was shocked by his response. He completely affirmed it, even though the man did not have good intentions for saying it. He warned me that with the opportunities to learn and grow that I would have, I had better be a better preacher than him.

My father was right. When my father was a young preacher, to use the biblical languages he had to learn the biblical languages. There was no Bible software to help him easily get to the meaning of Greek and Hebrew words. If my dad wanted to go to school, he had to go to school. Correspondence and online options for ministerial training were not available to him.

Resources my father could never have imagined are now available all around us. But we must take advantage of them. There is absolutely no excuse for any preacher to not be prepared to faithfully carry out the call to preach. Here are several helpful hints to consider as you prayerfully determine what training options and opportunities are best for you.

IF YOU CAN GO TO SEMINARY, DO IT

Not every preacher will have the opportunity to go off to seminary to prepare for ministry. But if you have the opportunity to go to seminary, by all means, do it. Of course, this is not a word from on high. And I understand that you must factor in your present family, work, and ministry responsibilities—not to mention the money. But if there seem to be green lights at these intersections, I would encourage you to prayerfully go forward and begin school.

There are some men who are very disciplined Bible students. And they are equipped for ministry through self-education. But most of us need the accountability and experience of actually being in a class, with all that requires. When you go into the pastorate, you become the resident theologian of your local church. You need to be a man of the Book to be a faithful pastor. And you need to learn how to exegete Scripture accurately to be a faithful preacher. So by all means, go if you can go. And do it before life, family, and ministry catches up to you.

SEMINARY DOES NOT MAKE
PASTORS AND PREACHERS

My father used to say that seminary just shines shoes. Guys who shine shoes do not make the shoes. They just shine them. If you don't bring a pair of shoes, they don't have anything to work with. Likewise, seminary does not make preachers. It doesn't make pastors. School can teach a man the biblical languages, systematic theology, church history, and even principles of Christian ministry. But if the Lord has not called you into His service, these things will not make you a pastor or a preacher.

Make sure you have a clear sense about the call of God on your life first. Get input from your pastor, congregation, family, and godly people you trust. If you are not clear about your call, wait. I would not advise you to go in order to figure out God's call. You may spend four years and end up even more confused! But if you have clarity about the Lord's call, go to school and prepare yourself the best you can for God (2 Timothy 2:15).

GO TO A BIBLE-BELIEVING SCHOOL

I know this may be hard for some of you to believe. Unfortunately, it's true. Some so-called Christian professors and schools do not believe the Bible. They spend more time trying to undermine its authority than teaching its message. So do your homework. And do not waste your time on any school that is not totally committed to the Bible. I don't care how famous or prestigious that school is. It is better to attend a small school where you will learn the Bible than to have a degree from some major institution that teaches liberal theology.

On that same note, I would not recommend that a pastor go to school to major in business, economics, computers, or other disciplines. Of course, this is between you and the Lord. But if the Lord has called you to be a herald of the Word or to shepherd the souls that He has purchased with His own blood, you should use the opportunity to focus on "the queen of the sciences"—theology!

BE A STUDENT—WHETHER OR NOT YOU ARE IN SCHOOL

Charles Haddon Spurgeon, the "Prince of Preachers," did not have formal training. In fact, he was not even formally ordained. He considered ordination to be the laying of empty hands on empty heads. Yet you would be hard pressed to find anyone who could match Spurgeon's mind for truth, preaching prowess, and pastoral vision.

True leaders are learners. Even if school is not for you now, keep studying. We really have no excuses these days for ignorance. As I mentioned earlier, for my father to learn the languages, systematic theology, and the other disciplines, he had to go to school. But we live in a day where there are so many resources available through various means. One of my favorite Bible teachers and authors admits that he is not a scholar in the languages, but he does know how to use the tools. And that would be my advice to you. You master a trade by learning how to use the tools. Remember, there are no better minds, just better libraries. Study hard and take every opportunity you are given to continue learning.

DO NOT GO TO SCHOOL JUST BECAUSE YOU WANT TO PASTOR

Many churches require at least a master's degree in their pastoral search process. This priority of having a prepared man is important and commendable. But it can also be misguided. A degree from a school does not tell you if a man has a godly character, a pastor's heart, or a gift to preach and teach. I know men who have finished their formal training, but have been unable to find an opportunity for pastoral ministry. And I know men who have not finished their formal training, but have been given opportunities to serve in the pastoral role. Ultimately, the Lord is the sovereign "Booking Agent" for pastors and preachers. He opens doors that no one can close and closes doors that no one can open. Trust the Lord to assign you where He wants you to be at the right time (Isaiah 40:28–31).

Chapter 3

FINDING TIME TO STUDY

I once had dinner with several pastors. As we waited for our table, a friend and new pastor asked, "How do you find time for study?" As soon as he finished the question, the hostess seated us. But when we sat down, he asked again, "So how do you find time for study, H. B.?" I thought about it for a minute. Then I offered several answers that I hope were helpful, and we moved on to other topics. But the question stayed with me.

Time management is one of the most crucial areas of stewardship in a pastor's life. We have lives and responsibilities outside of our pastoral duties, and the work of ministry is time consuming. We are always on call. Daily tasks demand our attention. Yet unexpected events throw our planned schedules into chaos.

Many people, including church members, think that pastors don't actually work. If only they knew the truth. In reality, most pastors feel overworked. Pastoral ministry is stressful. And if we are not careful, we can work so hard that we do not have time for our most important tasks: prayer and the ministry of the Word (Acts 6:4). As with many important matters in life, we don't have time to study. We must *make* time to study. Here are seven pieces of practical advice for maximizing your study time (plus one bonus point).

PLAN AHEAD

Your study time is already limited. You don't have time to figure out what you are going to preach each week. Your study time needs to be spent studying the text, not finding a text to study. So plan your preaching in advance. Planning ahead for a month or quarter or even a year will help you get down to business when it is time to study the text and prepare a message. The goal is to have a planned schedule that will enable you to use your time in study and make the most of it.

SCHEDULE YOUR STUDY TIME

Do you schedule meetings and appointments? How about your study time? Your time of study is just as important as staff meetings, counseling sessions, and hospital visits. So begin each week by marking out the hours you will study each day. Determine how long it takes to prepare a message. Schedule it into your week. Then keep your appointments to study and write. If you have a secretary, share your schedule with him or her and ask them to help you guard it. If not, be your own schedule security guard. Have the courage to tell people that you have something scheduled that you cannot cancel. And use that scheduled time to get your sermon work done.

STEAL TIME

There will be weeks when your schedule is out of control. Stealing time is a good way to make up for the time you may lose to other things. I copy down the resources that I need from week to week and put them in a file. I take it wherever I go, and I steal back as much time as I can while I am waiting for an appointment, between meetings, or any other time I can take advantage of. It may be only fifteen or twenty minutes. But those are minutes I can use to my advantage for Sunday. If you use software study tools, it is even easier for you to have your materials with you wherever you are. Make the most of any and every opportunity you get to study.

STUDY WHEN IT'S TIME TO STUDY

You know how it goes. When you finally get to the study, you are blitzed by the temptation to do other things. By all means, resist that temptation. When it's time to study, study. Don't web surf or answer emails or play with your smartphone or clean your desk or organize your books or . . . You get the point. Put your behind in the seat. Get to work. Don't procrastinate. Pray. Read. Study. Think. Write. You have no right to complain about the time you do not have if you do not use the time you have wisely. Remind yourself that you will never get this week again.

EDUCATE YOUR PEOPLE

Many church members think sermons grow on trees. They don't. Others think you just get up there and preach from the overflow of what you learned in seminary. You don't. At least, I hope you don't. Few church members understand what it takes to produce a good sermon. You must educate them. Talk to your deacons, elders, staff, leaders, and members about your study process. The more they understand what it takes for you to prepare, the more willing and able they will be to help you. Softhearted members will appreciate your labor, pray for your study, and free you up to prepare yourself to preach.

PRACTICE INTENTIONAL NEGLECT

Many urgent matters come across a pastor's desk each week. Much of it has nothing to do with prayer or the ministry of the

Word. You must distinguish between what is urgent and what is truly important, then learn to neglect some things during the week to prepare yourself for Sunday. Bottom line: You have failed if you go to every meeting, oversee every detail, and respond to every correspondence, but are not ready to preach. You will never get this Sunday again. Prioritize.

DELEGATE

In order to practice intentional neglect, without the sky falling around your ministry, make sure the things that need to be covered are covered by someone. If you have staff to assist you, trust them to do so. If you have to recruit and train volunteers, do it. Accept the fact that they may not do it the way you do it. Give them time to grow and room to fail. Stop trying to do it all. Determine the responsibilities that you can either give away or share. Then do it. And use the time you gain to work on your lesson for Wednesday and your sermon for Sunday.

BY ANY MEANS NECESSARY

Here is a bonus point: Do whatever you have to do to be ready to preach the Word of God and the testimony of Jesus Christ! View sermon preparation as spiritual warfare. There is a battle for your attention. The Enemy would do anything to keep you from spending time in the Word and preparing the message God wants your people to hear. Fight! Pray hard. Get up early. Sacrifice a night of sleep. Drink a cup of coffee. Turn off the TV. Sacrifice your favorite hobby until you are finished. Make deals to treat yourself for the amount of work you get done. Don't go to lunch until you've made some progress. Hold the calls and turn off the email alerts. Pass certain responsibilities on to others. Do whatever it takes to get ready to preach.

Chapter 4

DEVELOPING A SERMON CALENDAR

I believe in the Holy Spirit. Therefore, I plan my preaching in advance.

Some preachers inadvertently dishonor the Holy Spirit by thinking and acting as if His work is somehow quenched if He is not free to work spontaneously. They treat the Holy Spirit like a harried housewife, overwhelmed by a lazy husband, overactive kids, and dirty dishes and clothes who gets everything done just in the nick of time. This is foolish thinking. The Holy Spirit can lead just as effectively a year in advance as He can days in advance.

What an encouragement for developing a sermon calendar! God knows if there is going to be some tragedy that needs to be addressed. God knows when there will be a death that rocks the congregation. God knows if a crisis will arise in the church that will need attention. God knows what the individuals and families are going through in your congregation. God knows what you do not know! The fact that God knows our story from beginning to end means we need not specialize in "Saturday night specials." We can and should plan our preaching with confidence that God is at work in and through and beyond this process to ensure our congregations are shaped by the Word of God and the testimony of Jesus Christ.

There are several reasons why you should plan your preaching.

DEVOTING TIME TO SERMON PREPARATION

I am a sinner who needs to constantly watch his life and doctrine (1 Timothy 4:16). I am a husband and a father. I am a pastor with outside preaching responsibilities. And I am a human being who needs food, sleep, exercise, recreation, and fellowship. I simply cannot afford to wait until Thursday afternoon to determine what I am going to preach Sunday morning. I need to be able to redeem the time in my sermon preparation. This can only happen when I replace the time I would be spending each week thinking about what to preach with time thinking about the text and the sermon.

When you plan ahead, you can collect resources without the pressure of last-minute preparation. Because you know what you are going to be preaching on, you can scan your library for illustrative material in advance. You can have a mental trigger that notes things you may read in a blog, newspaper, or magazine that may be useful later on. You can scan the web for material related to your text or subject. And you can give your subconscious time to "marinate" in the text, deepening your thoughts and sharpening your creativity. You can also have an advantage when facing the busyness of life and "interruptions" of pastoral ministry. Having a sermon plan acts as a magnet to draw material together for your preaching.

SHEPHERDING THE CHURCH

Your preaching is the most effective way you can impact your congregation. Sunday morning is when you can touch the most people at one time. You must be a good steward of your opportunity. This happens by how you plan, not just by how you preach and study. You can easily end up at the rear of the parade if you wait until the end of the week to choose your text for Sunday. Your preaching will become too reactionary. By planning your preaching in advance, you can strategically lead your church forward in thinking and living biblically.

MAINTAINING DOCTRINAL BALANCE

In his farewell address to the Ephesian elders, Paul declared, "Therefore I testify to you this day that I am innocent of the blood of all, for I did not shrink from declaring to you the whole counsel of God" (Acts 20:26–27). This is how I want to end my ministry. So should you. But this cannot happen if you are only riding your theological hobbyhorses from week to week.

Your congregation needs a balanced diet of God's Word to grow in the grace and knowledge of Jesus Christ (2 Peter 3:18). They need to hear law and gospel. They need to be taught Christian doctrine and Christian living. They need to be exposed to the various forms of literature in the Old and New Testaments. Planning your preaching helps to guard against "vain repetition" in your preaching and establish a strategy for declaring the whole counsel of God.

PLANNING CORPORATE WORSHIP

The pastor is the worship leader of the church, whether he knows music or not. Hearing the Word of God is the highest form of worship. It also feeds the other elements of worship. Our worship will go higher only as we deepen our understanding of God's Word. Everything that happens in worship should be viewed as an extension of the teaching ministry of the church. Planning your preaching gives a pastor a practical tool to oversee corporate worship and to plan more meaningful times together in worship.

When the preaching has been planned ahead, you can assign appropriate Scripture readings that support the message. Music can be selected that highlights the theme of the message. Special, creative elements can be planned for the worship services. You can decide that everything in the service one Sunday will be on prayer. Or you can cross themes, preaching on the grace of God and singing about the holiness of God. Generally, your people should know what to regularly expect from the worship service. But every now and then you should knock their socks off with something special. Developing a sermon plan can be a great catalyst to accomplish this.

DEVELOPING A SERMON CALENDAR

There are different ways to develop a sermon calendar. Some pastors plan for the month ahead, ensuring that they will be at least several weeks ahead of the game. Others plan for the next quarter.

These are good places to start, but I recommend establishing a preaching calendar for a whole year. Planning your preaching for the year can make it easier to plan the rest of the program of your church. You can establish tools and goals and service opportunities to coincide with your preaching for the year. You can even organize Bible study groups around the Sunday morning preaching. This may seem like a daunting task. But it is not as hard as it sounds. You can start now and plan for the next twelve months. Pick a time and begin planning for the next calendar year. If your schedule permits, go away for several days and plan your preaching. Or schedule specific times during your regular routine when you will focus on this. Here are several practical suggestions for planning your preaching a year in advance.

START WITH PRAYER

Preaching the Word of God to the people of God is a sacred, serious task. You do not want to decide what to preach in a cavalier manner, which is why you should consider developing a sermon plan in the first place. Approach this process with a conscious sense of dependence upon God to lead and guide you.

Pray about potential books of the Bible, themes, or series to preach. What truths would the Lord have you teach your people in the coming year? Pray for and about your congregation. Pray about the spiritual condition of your congregation. Pray about their needs, individually and corporately. Pray about the future. What is your vision for the church? Pray for yourself. The things you have been studying personally and devotionally may become fodder for your pulpit work. Is there something you need to learn? I have found that the best way for me to learn a subject is to preach it. It forces me to study it diligently.

TALK TO YOUR TEAM

You may be the pastor of your congregation. But you are not the only person of influence the Lord has placed in the body life of that church. There may be associate pastors, church officers, or ministry leaders who have helpful recommendations for your preaching in the year to come. Or there may be nonofficial leaders whose opinion you value. There may even be new or young members you can talk to. Indeed, there is wisdom in having a multitude of counselors. Take advantage of the perspectives of godly people you trust to plan your preaching.

GO THROUGH THE CALENDAR

At this point, I print a blank monthly calendar for the coming twelve months. I then mark the holidays that fall on Sundays or Sundays related to special programs or campaigns. I also take note of the special days in the life of the church that will guide my preaching. For instance, our Prayer Emphasis Week is every January. I use two Sundays to preach on prayer. October is our Stewardship Emphasis Month, during which I will preach on financial stewardship.

I also put down the Sundays that I do not intend to preach. It is probably best that a pastor be in his own pulpit about forty-five Sundays of the year. But the hard number is not most important. What matters is that you plan when you will not preach. The bow that is always bent will soon break. You need to be delivered from the sweet bondage of weekly preparation occasionally. You may not be able to take an extended sabbatical, but at least arrange a mini-vacation from the pulpit. Use special days like church anniversaries or missions emphasis days to bring in a guest speaker. Recruit some of the young men around you. By any means necessary, take a break to recharge your batteries!

The biggest part of my sermon planning is choosing the series I am going to preach. My custom is to preach through books of the Bible. Consecutive exposition through books aids sermon planning. I pre-study the book enough to divide it into divisions I will preach. I may even pick a title for each sermon. I determine my start date, then start filling in the blanks in my calendar, skipping over holidays, special days, or Sundays I am out of the pulpit. The calendar fills up quickly.

Be flexible in this process. Like the Sabbath, the preaching plans are made for the preacher, not preachers for the preaching plan. Don't be a slave to a preaching calendar. If a natural disaster or tragedy takes place that should be addressed, do it. If there is an issue in your community or city that needs a Christian perspective, speak to it. If you are led for whatever reason to ditch your plan for a week or two to preach something else, by all means, do it.

Once you complete your sermon calendar, your work is not done. Review it continuously. Ask the Lord to edit in what He wants in and edit out what He wants out. The fact that plans may need to change is not a reason not to plan at all. Trust God to use your planning to strengthen your preaching, nurture your congregation, and honor the Scriptures. Remember, one who fails to plan, plans to fail.

Chapter 5

SERMON PREPARATION

"Do your best to present yourself to God as
one approved, a worker who has no need to be
ashamed, rightly handling the word of truth."

2 TIMOTHY 2:15

A pastor's primary responsibility is to preach and teach the Word of God and the testimony of Jesus Christ (2 Timothy 4:1–5). Faithfulness to this holy charge requires personal devotion, diligent study, and laborious preparation. Good preaching is hard work.

But how do you get from text to sermon? What steps should a preacher take to preach a sound, clear, and helpful sermon? The following steps are an overview of my process of sermon preparation. This is just one preacher's way of going about his work. It is not the only way to do it, and I am sure it is not the best way. But you may find it beneficial to compare another preacher's process of sermon preparation.

PRAY

First, start your sermon preparation with diligent prayer. Pray that the Lord would open your eyes to see wonderful things in the Word (Psalm 119:18). And pray that the Lord would give you understanding that you may keep His Word (Psalm 119:34). Do not let prayer become a perfunctory act. R. Kent Hughes said it well: "Sermon preparation is twenty hours of prayer." Saturate every part of your study with prayer. Pray that Christ would oversee your study. Trust the Holy Spirit to lead you to the truth. Seek the mind of God in the text. Repent as the text confronts you with sin in your life. Pray for wisdom as you read. Ask for clarity as you write. Work as if it all depends on you, but pray as if it all depends on God. I'll have more to say about the topic of prayer at the end of this section.

READ AND REREAD THE TEXT

Before you understand what a text means, you need to listen to what it says. You definitely won't understand 1 Corinthians if you don't actually read 1 Corinthians. So don't begin your study by crafting an outline before you have spent time reading the text. Read it prayerfully. Read it slowly. Read it carefully. Read it aloud. Mark it up as you read. Read expecting the text to speak to you. Then read the text again. And again. Saturate your mind with the text until it gets into your system. Let the Word of God speak to you before you try to speak the Word of God to others.

COMPARE TRANSLATIONS

You may study and preach from a particular translation. But it pays to read the text from several different versions. It can help you to see the text with fresh eyes. It will highlight words that need to be studied more, and it will further get the text into your heart and mind. Read the committee translations, like the New King James, New American Standard, English Standard Version, and the Holman Christian Standard Bible. Likewise, read some good paraphrases like *The Living Bible*, J. B. Phillips's paraphrase, or Eugene

Peterson's *The Message*. Get a parallel Bible that has multiple translations side by side. Another good tool is *The Bible from 26 Translations*. Reading from different translations will get you deeper into the text and will also help you see words, phrases, and sentences that you should focus on in your study.

OBSERVE THE TEXT

The inductive Bible study method asks four big questions of the text: (1) Observation asks, What does it say? (2) Interpretation asks, What does it mean? (3) Application asks, How does it apply? And (4) Correlation asks, How does it relate to the rest of Scripture? (See *Living by the Book: The Art and Science of Reading the Bible* by Howard and William Hendricks for a clear and comprehensive introduction to the inductive Bible study method.)

The process begins with Observation. In Observation, you are simply taking notes on what you see in the text. Start your formal study of the text with an open Bible, pen and paper (or computer keyboard). Just work through what you see in the text. Note important, repeated, or difficult words. Do sentence diagrams. Ask journalistic questions (who?, what?, when?, where?, and why?). Do sanctified brainstorming until you have thought yourself empty.

DO WORD STUDIES

You may not be an expert in the original languages, but with all of the study helps available, there is no excuse for you misreading the original words of the text. If possible, learn the languages through formal training. If that is not possible, determine to master the tools that help you understand the languages better.

As you work through the text, study word meanings, grammar, and usage. Find out what the word meant when the writer used it, not just the *Webster's Dictionary* meaning. And then make sure you are clear about what the word means in context. But don't drag all of this exegetical data into the pulpit. Put what you learn into clear, picturesque language so that you do not drown your people in unnecessary technical details.

REVIEW THE CROSS-REFERENCES

This is the Correlation part of the inductive Bible study method. You want to make sure your reading of the text lines up with what the rest of Scripture has to say on the subject. If you have an idea that cannot be backed up anywhere else in Scripture, you're wrong. So let Scripture interpret Scripture by carefully reviewing pertinent cross-references. Some may suggest themselves as you study, and there are helpful tools including topical Bibles (like *Nave's*) or handbooks like *The Treasury of Scripture Knowledge*.

READ THE COMMENTARIES

There is wisdom in a multitude of counselors. So take advantage of the wisdom of diligent Bible commentators. Don't treat commentators as if they are divinely inspired, but be humble enough to learn from the wisdom of others. Read exegetical commentaries for insights into the text. Read homiletical commentaries with a view toward shaping the text for the pulpit. Read devotional commentaries to get at the heart of the text for application. Read the commentaries to sharpen your thinking, not to do the thinking for you.

SURVEY ADDITIONAL SOURCES

Thank God for the Internet! There are many church and ministry websites where sermon outlines, manuscripts, and audio messages are posted. Likewise, there are books of sermons, which may have a chapter on the text you are working on. And there are sermon tapes, CDs, and mp3s you can pick up to hear how different preachers have dealt with your text. Take advantage of these resources to broaden your thinking as you prepare your message. But don't let these take the place of your message or your own thinking and preparing.

DEVELOP A SERMON SKELETON

A "sermon skeleton" is a statement of your sermon's purpose, aims, and structure. This is where you put your study material together in sermonic form. Pick a title. Identify the doctrinal theme of the message. State the point, thesis, or big idea of the sermon in a single sentence. Work through the objectives for the sermon (what do you want the hearer to think, feel, do?). Craft your outline. Write out your transitional sentences. Put the structure together before you try to put meat on the bones.

WRITE A COMPLETE SERMON MANUSCRIPT

If you develop your sermon skeleton carefully, you may be tempted to slap an introduction and conclusion on it and declare yourself ready to preach. Resist that temptation. Take the time to write out a complete, word-for-word manuscript. This will help you think through and fully develop your ideas, and allow you to absorb the sermon into your memory. You may not take the manuscript to the pulpit. In fact, I recommend you don't. You should prepare a brief set of notes for preaching. But these pulpit notes should be pared down from a complete sermon manuscript. In summary, your sermon process should consist of several practical steps: Think yourself empty. Read yourself full. Write yourself clear. And pray yourself hot. Then go to the pulpit and be yourself. But don't preach yourself—preach Jesus to the glory of God!

Chapter 6

WHY I PRAY
BEFORE I PREACH

I preached my first sermon as a boy, eleven years old. The first thing I did when I stood up was pray. No one instructed me to do this. My father never prayed when he stood to preach. And none of the preachers I regularly heard or looked up to prayed at the beginning of their sermons. For some reason, I did. I had a clear sense of a call to preach, but I was scared out of my wits. Saying a prayer helped me to get on with it that day. It still does.

After observing this practice several times, a more seasoned pastor advised me, "If you haven't prayed before you stand up to preach, it's too late. And if you have already prayed, it's not necessary." He was absolutely right. I couldn't argue with his logic. Yet I continued to pray before I read my Scripture and began my sermon. And I still do to this day.

Let me be clear. I am not saying this is what you ought to do, if it is not your practice. And it is not a negative statement about your preaching if you do not begin it with a public prayer. This is not a measure of one's spirituality. Whether a preacher does this is not a moral issue. No one is right or wrong here. But I do believe it is good and healthy to publicly pray before you preach. There are two reasons.

TO SPEAK FAITHFULLY

The call to preach has been a part of the Lord's sanctifying work in my life. The responsibility of preaching to others has been a means by which the Lord has kept my mind and heart close to Him. My great sense of neediness in private study and public speaking drive me to God in prayer. And this sense of dependence grows the closer I get to the preaching moment. As the time to preach nears, I am more sensitive to the reality of my sins and sinfulness. I feel a great sense of unworthiness. It blows me away to think that God would use someone like me to do something as important as preach the Word. Even when I feel good about my preparation and think I have a pretty good sermon, there is still no room for pride. Without the Lord's sufficient grace and perfecting strength (2 Corinthians 12:9), I know my preaching is doomed to fail. Nothing good could come out of my standing behind the pulpit without God's help.

I understand what Paul meant when he spoke of preaching with weakness, fear, and trembling (1 Corinthians 2:3). But when I finish with my pulpit prayer, I am ready to preach. The anxiety goes away. And I am able to get on with the assignment the Lord has entrusted to me. Prayer reminds me that it is all in the hands of the Lord. I can only plant or water the seed. It is the Lord who causes the seed to grow.

On the other hand, there are times when I have to fight my ego from getting engaged in the preaching moment. But this is not because I come to the pulpit thinking I am such a great preacher. Usually, it is just the opposite. I often feel a great sense of insecurity before I preach. I am prone to think too much about what the congregation will think about the sermon. Or me. There can rise up something in me that makes me want the congregation to think I can really preach.

This is pride, a dangerous form of it. It is easy to justify pulpit pride by thinking that you just want to give God your best in the pulpit. Next thing you know, you can lose sight of who is to be lifted up in the sermon—Christ or the preacher. I am conscious of this sinful temptation of pride. So I pray before I preach. Prayer humbles me, clarifies my focus, and sets my heart on the sacred task of preaching the Word of God and the testimony of Jesus Christ.

FOR THE CONGREGATION TO HEAR CLEARLY

I believe there is a reason why Jesus often said, "He who has ears to hear, let him hear" (Matthew 13:9; Mark 4:9; Revelation 2:7). Just because you have ears does not mean you can hear the truth. Hearing is a spiritual act, not a physical one. It is a miracle that is wrought by the power of God. Without the work of the Holy Spirit to convince and convict, the sinful ear will dismiss the sermon as mere human opinion, rather than the Word of God. So I pray that the Lord would cause the good seed of the Word to fall on good ground that will bear fruit to His glory.

I also pray publicly so that the congregation will recognize that the preaching and hearing of the Word of God is serious business, and they will be held accountable for what they hear. The sermon is not a performance for the congregation to enjoy. It is to be a mirror that causes them to see themselves as God sees them. I want the congregation to take the message as seriously as I do when I deliver it. Only God can transform an indifferent audience into a waiting congregation that is ready to trust and obey the Word of truth.

"Open my eyes," prayed the psalmist, "that I may behold wondrous things out of your law" (Psalm 119:18). There are wonderful things in the Word of God that will be missed if our eyes are not open. Sin closes our eyes to these wonderful things. The various situations that hurt, trouble, or burden the congregation can also close their eyes to the truth. And Satan is at work to close the eyes of believers and unbelievers alike in the congregation, so that they will not see their need for a Savior and the sufficiency of the person and work of Jesus Christ.

Even in the corporate worship of the living God, there are myriad distractions that can pull a person's attention away from the preaching of the Word. Their bodies can be in the room while their minds can be on the other side of town. Even the previous elements of the worship service can be distracting if they are not planned and executed with spiritual excellence. There are so many things that happen before I stand up to preach that work against the message.

So I begin the sermon with a word of prayer. I pray for myself and for the congregation. I pray with the confidence that God is at work through my prayers, not just the sermon. I believe that as I pray, God helps me to speak the Word faithfully and clearly. And I believe God helps the congregation to hear in a way that will lead to repentance, faith, and obedience. I have seen the Lord do it too many times to believe otherwise.

Chapter 7

WHAT I PRAY
BEFORE I PREACH

Father, please give me the physical strength and spiritual energy to speak your Word with faithfulness, clarity, authority, passion, wisdom, humility, and liberty."

These are words I often pray as I lead the congregation in prayer before I read my text and begin my sermon. I do not know when I started praying this prayer, and I don't remember forming these words intentionally. But they have become a regular part of my praying before I preach.

This prayer is no magical mantra. And I do not pray it out of vain repetition. I pray this because I need the Lord to do the same thing for me every time I stand to preach. Whether I pray this publicly or privately, these are seven things I want the Lord to do in and through me as I preach.

FAITHFULNESS

I want to obey the divine command to preach the Word (2 Timothy 4:2). This requires that I understand the meaning of the text. Then I must prepare and present a message that submits to the authorial intent of the text. I want to bring out of the text what's in the text, rather than imposing my own ideas upon it. I want my thoughts and words to be consistent with sound doctrine. In a word, I want my preaching to be faithful.

The sermon is not my message. The congregation members are not my people. And the preaching moment is not my time. I am on assignment as a herald for the King. I am on kingdom business. "This is how one should regard us, as servants of Christ and stewards of the mysteries of God," said the apostle Paul. "Moreover, it is required of stewards that they be found faithful" (1 Corinthians 4:1–2). But the steward cannot do this in his own strength. He needs divine help. So I pray the Lord would help me to be faithful in my preaching.

CLARITY

Paul often asked the churches to pray for him. And a top prayer request was that he would have clarity as he proclaimed the message of Christ (Ephesians 6:19–20). Clarity is essential for faithful preaching. What good is it to get the text right if you cannot make the text clear? You do not want the light in your study to become a fog in the pulpit. So you should pray that the Lord would give you clarity in preaching.

One of the best compliments a person can give me is to say that my preaching is clear. I do not want the listener to be confused about what I am saying. The person in the pew will not agree with everything I say. I accept that. But I want the explanation of the text and the point of the message to be clear. I don't want to be so deep that I drown the congregation. I want the congregation to clearly understand what God is saying in the text. I also believe that clarity is a virtue in its own right. There is something attractive about a message that is clear. So I pray that the sermon I write and the message I preach will be clear.

AUTHORITY

When I began my first pastorate as a teenager, I had no personal authority to draw from. At my installation, the late Dr. E. V. Hill preached a classic sermon entitled "What Can That Boy Tell Me?" His point was that I had the authority to preach whatever the Word of God says. I quickly learned that truth is truth whether I experience it or not. The Word of God stands on its own without needing my life to validate it.

The preacher's ultimate authority is found in the Word of God. The congregation really does not need to hear about my experience as a father or husband. My experience does not carry divine authority. What the Word of God says is infinitely more important than my testimonials. So I want to preach with biblical authority that reflects the fact that the text is the Word of God, not the words of man. And I pray that what I preach and how I preach will reflect and emphasize the exclusive authority of the Word of God.

PASSION

Many newscasters advocate a position rather than present the news. This turns me off. But this is exactly what should happen in preaching. I do not want to preach like a news reporter who is dispassionately reading copy from a teleprompter. I want my preaching to reflect a head and heart that have been gripped by the truth. Passionate preaching is not about gestures, volume, and emotion. It's about deep conviction, blood earnestness, and holy reverence. The people in the pew may not believe what I am saying. But I want it to be evident that *I* believe it. If preaching is "logic on fire," we should preach with convinced minds and enflamed hearts. We should pray that God would set us on fire in the pulpit and that we will burn with passion for His glory.

WISDOM

"Him we proclaim," said Paul, "warning everyone and teaching everyone with all wisdom, that we may present everyone mature in Christ" (Colossians 1:28). Wisdom should mark our preaching. Of course, the content of our preaching should reflect the wisdom of God, rather than the foolishness of the world. Likewise, we need wisdom for the presentation of the Word. Wisdom will guide us as to what to say and how to say it. Pray that the Lord would give you wisdom in preaching to comfort the afflicted and afflict the comfortable.

HUMILITY

The preaching moment is not about you. We are called to preach Jesus and not ourselves (2 Corinthians 4:5). It is impossible to exalt Christ and exalt self at the same time. We are just friends of the Groom, like John the Baptist (John 3:29). We must decrease that Christ may increase (John 3:30). Our job is to preach in such a way that brings the hearer before the living God. Then we are to get out of the way! But our sinful flesh will constantly seek to be in the spotlight. Prayer helps to keep our egos in check. Prayer helps us to remember who and what the preaching moment is about. Prayer helps us to preach with a humility that makes much of Christ and little of ourselves.

LIBERTY

I recently began to pray this after reading a biography of an influential preacher of the last century. In letters to supporters, he would often ask them to pray that he would have liberty when he preached. That stuck with me. I don't know how to explain it, but anyone who has been preaching for a while knows what it is like to preach with liberty and what it is to preach without it. There are times you stand to preach, and it feels like you are in one of those driver's education cars. Someone is putting their foot on the brakes, while you put your foot on the gas. But there are other times when God is obviously present and actively in charge of the preaching moment. And you can feel the Lord guiding your thoughts, leading your words, and moving the congregation. I want to feel that every time I preach. So I ask for freedom to preach my heart and convictions to the glory of God.

What do you pray before you preach?

Part 2:

THE PRACTICE
OF PREACHING

Chapter 8

USING SCRIPTURE
IN PREACHING

Christian preaching is biblical preaching. We are charged to preach the Word of God to the people of God (2 Timothy 4:1–2). At the least, this solemn charge of biblical preaching means that our preaching should be focused on and filled with the truth, wisdom, and message of the Scriptures. Of course, just because a man reads, quotes, and talks about the Bible in his sermon does not mean he is preaching the Word. Many use the Word of God as a springboard to proclaim a self-styled, man-centered message that actually opposes the Word of God in the name of preaching. But it is clear that you cannot preach the Word if you do not actually use the Word in your preaching.

I hate it when I hear a preacher who seems to know more about sports, politics, entertainment, business, pop culture, or whatever, than he does about the text he has chosen as the basis of his sermon. Preachers should be men of one book. We should preach the authority of the Scriptures, not the opinion of man.

A certain pastor was known for being positive minded, never criticizing other preachers. After a disastrous sermon, several young preachers sought him out to see what he thought about it. "At least he had a good text," was his response. Indeed, the text is the best part of any sermon. Every sermon we preach should be saturated with the Word of God. Here are several practical ways you should use Scripture in preaching.

READ THE SCRIPTURES

"Until I come," instructed Paul, "devote yourself to the public reading of Scripture, to exhortation, to teaching" (1 Timothy 4:13). The reading of Scripture is an essential element of Christian worship and preaching. Don't just refer to a passage and launch into the sermon. Read the text. Read slowly, clearly, and meaningfully. I would advise that you make it a practice to read as much of the text as you are going to preach. Lay the Word of God before them and then expound on it.

It is my custom to begin the sermon with the reading of Scripture, rather than introducing the subject first and then mentioning the text. I even ask the congregation to stand with me as I read the text, in reverence for the author of the Word (Nehemiah 8:1–6). Whatever your pulpit custom may be, let the reading of the text reflect that the Word of God is the final authority of your preaching.

EXPLAIN THE SCRIPTURES

There are those who draw a hard distinction between preaching and teaching. But this dichotomy cannot be backed up by Scripture. In the same verse that Paul charges Timothy to preach the Word, he bids him to do so with "complete patience and teaching" (2 Timothy 4:2). Preaching and teaching go together. To preach the Word requires teaching the Word. So we should not be hesitant about having heavy doses of explanation in our preaching.

Woe to the congregation whose preacher never shows them the meaning of the text beyond the obvious things they can see for themselves. At the other end of this extreme, the pulpit is not a seminary classroom. Faithful preaching must explain the text—the words, grammar, context, background, and theological significance of the text. If your congregation does not leave with a better understanding of what the text means over and above what they can read for themselves, you have not done your job.

APPLY THE SCRIPTURES

Faithful preaching should not only show the congregation what the text means, it should also show them how it works. It should answer the question, "So what?" At its bare minimum, preaching should involve explanation and exhortation. We should call upon the hearer to shape their thinking and behavior by the Word of God (James 1:22).

I do not believe we have to make the Word of God "relevant." It already is. Our preaching should make the relevance of Scripture clear. We should preach with the conviction that the Bible is given to us for our transformation, not just information. Head knowledge without life change is spiritual hypocrisy. So work hard to impress upon your hearers the commands to obey, promises to trust, and truths to believe as they are revealed in the text.

CORRELATE THE SCRIPTURES

If your interpretation of the text cannot be supported by any other passage in Scripture, you are wrong. Period. Your preaching should be clearly consistent with the larger message of the Bible. As you let Scripture interpret Scripture, it will reinforce the meaning of one passage by demonstrating that it is consistent with what

Scripture teaches in other places. And it carries the authority of the Scriptures. I recommend buying *The Treasury of Scripture Knowledge*. It is a big book of cross-references. Look them up and examine how the rest of Scripture relates to your text. Use clarifying cross-references to shed light on the passage.

I like to argue by the preponderance of the evidence. If you will not accept what this text is saying, let me show you that Genesis, Psalms, and Matthew agree with what I am saying about this text. This is what scholars have called "the analogy of Scripture." Scripture is its own best interpreter. Learn to put your Bible together in preaching, showing how one truth relates to another.

ILLUSTRATE WITH THE SCRIPTURES

Homileticians warn aspiring preachers to craft illustrations from life rather than using illustration books. I understand the reasoning behind this advice. But I wholeheartedly disagree. My advice would be to find illustrations from wherever you can, including illustration books. If you get one or two good ones from a three-hundred-page illustration book, I think it was worth the price of the volume.

But the best advice I can give you is to find illustrations in Scripture. As you are illustrating with Scripture, it will have the authority of God behind it. Likewise, you can continue to teach as you are illustrating. We are preaching to an increasingly biblically illiterate generation. Many who sit in our pews did not grow up in Sunday school and do not know the great stories of the Bible. Using Scripture to illustrate is an opportunity for us to use the Scriptures to illustrate and instruct at the same time. It permits you to teach and illustrate and keeps the sermon focused on the Word of God and the testimony of Jesus Christ.

Chapter 9

SELECTING A
TEXT TO PREACH

W hat should I preach?

This is a question the preacher will repeatedly ask himself. This question will also come with a sense of urgency, as time steadily marches toward the next preaching assignment. But the answer is not always easy.

Young preachers struggle with the question of what to preach. You may not get to preach regularly. Worse, you may not know *when* you are going to preach. You want to make the best of the opportunities you have. Likewise, seasoned pastors also struggle with the question of what to preach. You may have preached to the same congregation for years, and you do not want your preaching to become stale. Yet you feel like you have covered the major texts and themes of Scripture. You want to stay fresh in the pulpit, and that's what your congregation wants too.

What should you preach? What should you preach this Sunday? What should you preach over the next few weeks? What should you preach for the special event you have been invited to? My first piece of advice would be to start with a text. Whenever possible, anchor your preaching to a specific text that you explain and apply. Here are several ways to find what text is best for the occasion, whatever it may be.

PRAY

This is not a trite answer. Prayer is essential to the selection of a text, just as much as it is vital to the study process and sermon preparation. Go to God in prayer and ask Him to guide you for what you should preach. Ask for clear direction. Seek God diligently. Trust the promise that God will generously give wisdom to those who ask for it in faith (James 1:5–8). Indeed, you want to do a good job when you preach. But your concern for the preaching moment can never match God's. His name, Word, and glory are at stake when you preach. So pray and ask the Lord to lead you in selecting a text for preaching, with confidence that God will hear and answer your prayer.

PROCLAIM CHRIST

Christian preachers are ministers of the new covenant (2 Corinthians 3:5–6). We are ambassadors for Christ (2 Corinthians 5:20). We are witnesses for the Lord Jesus (Acts 1:8). As such, our preaching should focus on the person and work of Jesus Christ. Select texts that clearly present the truth about Christ. Preach the Gospels. Go to the Epistles and select one of the great texts that focus on Christ. Lift passages from the Old Testament that promise the coming of Christ and point to Him. Do not fear that people will know all of these passages and not want to hear them. The fact is, people do not know enough about Christ. And if your people get tired of hearing about Jesus, that is all the more reason to preach Him.

CHOOSE CLEAR TEXTS

If you are going to preach on a specific theme or subject, choose a text that is clearly about the subject you want to preach. Maybe you want to preach on prayer. Great! You will have a lot of fine texts to preach. But do not choose some obscure text that is not really about prayer. Don't force a subject on a text where it does not belong. And don't pick a passage where prayer is the secondary, passing subject and treat it like it is the primary theme of the text. You abuse the Scriptures when you preach the right truth from the wrong text. Faithful preaching keeps the main thing of the text the main thing.

PRACTICE VARIETY

Though I am relatively short, I was pretty good at basketball. I was quick and sharp on the court. I had a good jump shot. And I could pass the ball well. But my best weapon is that I am left-handed. Defenders did not know how to play me. But once a guy made me go to my right, I was done. To overcome this I had to learn to dribble to my right. Preaching is the same way. The temptation is to select texts that play to your strengths. But when we only preach the passages we are familiar or comfortable with, we rob our listeners. Stretch yourself. Pick texts that will force you to work and think and grow. Do you preach often from the Epistles? Try an Old Testament narrative. Do you spend a lot of time in the Gospels? Try a couple of Psalms. Keep forcing yourself to dribble with your off hand.

KNOW YOUR LIMITS

"All Scripture is breathed out by God" (2 Timothy 3:16). But you are not ready to preach every Scripture. There are some theological matters that you have yet to work through. And to preach on those subjects would only confuse people. There are genres of Scripture that you do not know how to handle well. There are spiritual issues in texts that you are wrestling with in your own life. These are not reasons to avoid certain passages altogether, but they do require that you be honest with yourself. Are you ready to preach this text? Have you spent enough time on this subject? Are there certain doctrinal convictions you need to work through before you can treat that text fairly? Do you need to repent of a sin before you get up and challenge others to live faithfully in that same area? Be honest with yourself. Know your limits. Choose texts that you can preach faithfully as you grow in faith, experience, and maturity.

While you must recognize your limitations, strive to proclaim the whole counsel of God. When I used to play basketball, I would often cherry-pick. Do you know what that is? It means when the other guys on my team were playing defense, I would sit under our basket and wait for the ball so I could get an easy bucket. But this only works for so long. At some point, both your team and the other team will figure out what you are doing. The same is true in preaching. You cannot spend your entire ministry cherry-picking. You can't win if you just sit under the basket, waiting to get an easy shot. You have to play both sides of the ball. You must preach the whole counsel of God, which often involves stretching and challenging yourself in new directions. You should give your people a comprehensive diet of God's Word. This is why I believe exposition through entire books is the most faithful way to preach over the long haul, as we'll see in the next chapter. Of course, you cannot preach the entire Bible in depth. But you can preach the major themes and texts of the Bible. Factor that goal into your selection of texts. Strive to tell the truth, the whole truth, and nothing but the truth.

Chapter 10

CONSECUTIVE EXPOSITION

"People have short attention spans," it is claimed. "You cannot do long series through books anymore. People will check out on you after four sermons. Six, at the most."

This common claim is simply not true. People are hungry for the Word of God. They do not always recognize the nature of their hunger. But whether they know it or not, people need to know the Word of God. "Man shall not live by bread alone," said Jesus, "but by every word that comes from the mouth of God" (Matthew 4:4). Consecutive exposition both satisfies people's hunger for Scripture and shapes it. Bible exposition is an acquired taste. Before people experience it, they don't know what they are missing. But once they do, they will not be satisfied with anything else.

Consecutive exposition is not the only way to preach faithfully. Jesus did not preach that way. Charles Spurgeon, the Prince of Preachers, did not preach consecutively through Scripture. My father was a strong and faithful preacher. But he did not preach in series, much less do consecutive exposition. Yet I contend that consecutive exposition—preaching through a book of the Bible from beginning to end—is the most faithful way to preach.

Many preachers reject consecutive exposition for various reasons. I believe the main issue may simply be that it's hard work. It is not for the slothful. But the hard work of consecutive exposition is worth the effort for the following reasons.

LEADS TO BETTER
UNDERSTANDING OF THE WORD

As pastors, we encourage our people to read through the Bible, convinced that it is essential for their growth in Christ (2 Timothy 3:16–17). Many of the Bible reading plans we use are organized to help us read through Scripture. Why do we hesitate to study and preach this way? We rob ourselves when we treat Scripture as a topical reference guide. The Bible is not an encyclopedia that you only reference when you are looking for specific, predetermined information. It is a love letter that you pore over slowly and carefully. It is to our benefit to follow the complete train of thought of a text in its context, rather than lifting selected verses at our discretion.

MODELS CONTEXTUAL BIBLE STUDY

We study the text in private to prepare to preach in public. We also model how to study as we preach to the congregation. The way we handle Scripture in the pulpit exemplifies to our people how to study the Bible, for good or bad. A constant diet of random verses gives the wrong impression about how to approach Scripture. There is nothing wrong with looking to the Bible for answers to topics. But you should also let the Bible raise the questions through texts. You should let the Bible lead the conversation. You should let the Bible determine the subjects that matter. Consecutive exposition is a platform to demonstrate proper and consistent Bible interpretation.

PREVENTS OVEREMPHASIZING
FAVORITE TOPICS

All Scripture is God-breathed. Yet there are passages, sections, and books that grip us more tightly. We all have particular books of the Bible we enjoy preaching and teaching. We gravitate toward select doctrines. Certain subjects light our fire. But these must not be the extent of the menu we feed our people. As I contended in the previous chapter, we must declare the whole counsel of God (Acts 20:26–27). Consecutive exposition ensures your congregation is properly exposed to the unfamiliar texts, obscure personalities, and unpopular truths of the Bible they need to hear.

DEMONSTRATES THE
SUFFICIENCY OF SCRIPTURE

The previous century saw the battle for the Bible waged in the church. Faithful Christians took a stand to defend the inspiration and inerrancy of Scripture. Yet the battle for the credibility of Scripture continues. The battlefield is no longer biblical inspiration. It is now a fight over the sufficiency of Scripture. There are many pastors and churches that would readily affirm the Bible is the Word of God. But they turn to everything but Scripture to reach the lost, disciple the saints, lead the church, counsel the troubled, and impact the culture. We lack a true confidence in the Word of God. We almost apologize for it, constantly seeking to "make it relevant." But if Scripture is not inherently relevant, you cannot make it so. Preaching through a book of the Bible can demonstrate the fundamental relevance of Scripture to your congregation as you tackle neglected texts that teach life-changing truths.

FORCES YOU TO ADDRESS DIFFICULT
SUBJECTS AND PASSAGES

Without consecutive exposition, there are important truths and themes we will never preach. Some texts we avoid, and we never think to address certain subjects. But working through a book of the Bible causes you to cover neglected but important truths. It also protects you from the accusation that you are meddling when you have to challenge or warn your people in your sermons. If a difficult word is preached, your defense is that you were only working with the text that was in front of you. It would be irresponsible to skip over something you would rather not say. Faithfulness requires you to play the ball where it lies. Consecutive exposition gives you a platform and the authority to preach the truth, the whole truth, and nothing but the truth.

MAKES IT EASY TO PLAN
YOUR PREACHING IN ADVANCE

How can you be consistent and effective on Sunday morning if you don't know what you are going to preach on until Thursday? As we saw in chapter 4, you need to have a plan for planning your preaching. An intentional preaching schedule allows you to get an early start or even work ahead. Consecutive preaching is ideal for sermon planning. Start by outlining the book for preaching. Determine, as best you can, how many messages you will preach from that particular book. Then as you begin your series, move on to the next text from week to week. What if you are led to preach something else in the process? By all means, do it. Humbly follow when the Lord leads you away from your plan on a special occasion. Then get back to your exposition and take advantage of the extra time having a preaching schedule gives you.

HELPS BUILD AN EXPOSITORS LIBRARY

Faithful expositors need strong tools to do good pulpit work. You need an expositors library. If you are a new pastor, you probably cannot afford to aggressively build your library. You have to do it slowly, carefully, and strategically. In that regard, jumping from text to text can be expensive if you try to secure helpful research tools. But as you preach consecutively through a book, you can select the best available works. Work through them as you preach the book. And wait to secure other materials until preparation for the next series requires it. This way you can build up a library of tools over time that will serve you well throughout your ministry.

Chapter 11

BECOMING A
BETTER EXPOSITOR

I received a message from someone who heard me speak at a preaching conference. He thanked me for my ministry and encouraged me to remain faithful. He also had a question: What advice would you give to help me become a better expositor?

What a great question!

I am a student of expository preaching, not an expert. But I relish the opportunity to answer questions like this. My heart's desire is to be a better preacher. I trust that my preaching is clear and consistent from week to week. Yet I recognize that I still have much to learn about the great task of Bible exposition. We all do.

I pray this will always be my disposition. No preacher should ever feel he has arrived. We all have weaknesses in our preaching. We all have growing to do. We all have blind spots that cannot be seen without trusted people being honest with us. But those blind spots are there, whether or not we identify them or acknowledge them. We should actively seek them out and strive to address them. We have already noted some of what follows in chapter 5, but it bears repeating and elaborating on. Here is what I would recommend to a preacher—rookie or seasoned—who seeks to become a better expositor.

START EARLY

First, start early. There is a difference between what is important and what is urgent. At the beginning of the week, many urgent things claim your attention. All the while, the text for Sunday sits there quietly. You ignore it until the weekend approaches. Then it becomes both urgent and important! Yet you are not able to give it your best because you are operating on limited time. One practical way to avoid the Saturday-night-special syndrome is to start as early as possible. Many times, you will only have one opportunity to preach a given text. You should want to treat it right and preach it faithfully. To do so, you must use your study time wisely. This stewardship of time starts by getting to work as early as possible.

READ REPEATEDLY

Don't begin your study by glancing over the text and rushing to find an opportunity. Don't rush to the exegetical process too fast. And please don't start by consulting commentaries. Start your study of the Word of God with the Word of God. Before you study the text, read it. I mean, really read it. Then read it again. Read it slowly. Read it aloud. Read it from different translations. Read it prayerfully. Read it with expectation that God is speaking in and through the text. Read it devotionally. Meditate on the truths you are learning. Internalize the message of the text. Reading the text this way will help you become more familiar with the details and language of it. Moreover, there is great power in simply reading the Word of God. By simply reading the text, the Holy Spirit can and will reveal truth that you cannot glean any other way.

OBSERVE CAREFULLY

Bible exposition explains the meaning and message of the text. Therefore, proper interpretation is key. But so is observation. Interpretation asks, What does it mean? Observation asks, What does it say? Before you rush to determine the meaning of the text, pay attention to what is being said.

The tools of observation are a Bible, pen, and paper. Or it may be a Bible and computer. But don't use anything else at this point. Just read and write (or type) what you see. Analyze the words. Note the grammar. Diagram sentences. Look for repeated terms. Relate the passage to its context. Ask diagnostic questions. Mark connecting ideas. List words to look up. Note people and places to know. Review the cross-references. Meditate on the themes of the text. Make preliminary outlines. Don't stop until you've thoroughly investigated the text. I call this process "sanctified brainstorming." When I do it well, it is often the most fruitful part of my study. The more time you spend in observation, the more it will strengthen your interpretation.

DIG DEEP

There are no better minds, only better libraries. So consult the best resources available to you. Some will tell you not to put much stock in commentaries. I think this advice is foolish and arrogant. There are men and women who have spent years studying certain books of the Bible. Their life work has then been placed in commentaries. The least I can do is read their insights. Consider it consulting godly friends for spiritual advice. Some of my best friends are commentators whom I have never met. Some are no longer living. I read as much as I can—exegetical commentaries, homiletical commentaries, and even devotional commentaries. I want to dig as deeply as possible to gain all the insights that I can on the text.

READ WIDELY

For most pastors, it is a challenge spending adequate time studying for Sunday along with all of the other personal and ministerial responsibilities we have. This often crowds out time for personal reading. But there are some things you will never have time for. You must make time for them. Reading is one of them. I am convinced that the more you read in general, the more it will strengthen your pulpit work. Read theology, biography, Christian living, popular books, and even a little mental "junk food." Read blogs, journals, magazines, and newspapers. Read sermons by other preachers. Reading widely encourages critical thinking, sharpens your focus, encourages your faith, models good writing, and broadens your perspective.

WRITE CLEARLY

I am a proponent of writing complete sermon manuscripts, whether you take it to the pulpit or not. Diligent study can result in flat sermons if you do not think through what you want to say and how you want to say it. It is not enough to have an outline and then basically wing it from there. Write yourself clear. Craft your introduction. Work through your transitional sentences. Plan your conclusions. Select meaningful illustrations. Find effective cross-references. Construct compelling sentences. Help listeners to see what you are talking about. Most often, this cannot happen extemporaneously. It must be prepared beforehand. Strive to prepare a sermon that is worthy of the truth God has taught you from the text.

PRAY FERVENTLY

I mention prayer last, but it is certainly not least. It is essential to growing as a preacher. Believing prayer should mark your entire study and preparation process. Do not just check in with God at the beginning of your study time. Pray throughout your sermon process.

Ask God for wisdom (James 1:5). Ask God to grant the wisdom of the writers to you. Ask Him for understanding when you get stuck. Ask God to renew your mind and change your heart by what you study. Ask for a way to present the truth that will arrest the attention of your hearers. Ask God to help you decrease that Christ may increase. Ask for relevant applications for your congregation. Ask God the Holy Spirit to grip the hearts of your people. Ask God to give them increase, as you plant and water the good seed of the Word (1 Corinthians 3:6–8). Ask for physical strength and spiritual energy for the preaching moment. Ask God to glorify Himself through the proclamation of the Word. Prayer will ready your heart, sanctify your life, guide your study, clarify your message, and strengthen your preaching. Praying preachers are strong, healthy, and growing.

Chapter 12

SERMON OUTLINES

Every sermon should have a destination. It also needs a clear path to get there. A sermon outline charts the path for the sermon to reach its intended destination.

Good sermons have effective outlines. Of course, a sermon is more than an outline, but it is not less. The outline gives structure to the message. That structure supports the substance of the message. Your body is much more than a skeleton, yet it is built on and around the connecting bones of the skeleton.

There are different philosophies about the use of outlines in sermons. There is an inductive approach to preaching that is gaining popularity in which the preacher holds the point of the message until the end. Many others still maintain a more traditional approach that states the key point up front and uses the outline to support the thesis in the body of the message.

I am an advocate of the traditional approach. Tell them what you are going to say. Say it. Then tell them what you said. I believe this is the method that best facilitates Bible exposition and the teaching of Scripture. Yet there are different ways this can be carried out in preaching.

I regularly state the points of the sermon for the congregation as

I preach. Sometimes I state them all at the end of the introduction, as I transition to the main body. This gives an overview of where the sermon is going before you get too far into it. But I most often announce the movements one by one as I go, hoping to build a sense of suspense and momentum as the sermon progresses. But this is not the only way to do it. I never heard my father refer to the "points" of his sermon. His style was more conversational. He simply worked his way through the body of the message without making any reference to its underlying structure. He knew where he was going. And the listener followed along without obvious sermon highway signs.

Whether you formally state your points or not, you ought to know where you are going with the sermon. And you should preach it in a way that gives the congregation confidence that you know where you are going.

How are good sermon outlines developed? What are the characteristics of a compelling outline? Here are ten practical tips to help you be more effective in developing sermon outlines.

LET THE TEXT SHAPE THE OUTLINE

How many points should a sermon have? As many or as few as the text requires. Period. Don't force an arbitrary outline on the text. Don't use the text as a jumping-off spot for predetermined points you want to make. And don't mention a text and then go into all the world preaching the gospel. The goal of biblical preaching is to let the text speak for itself. And the text does not always communicate its truth in three points. Your outline should amplify the message of the text.

PREACH THE TEXT, NOT THE OUTLINE

It is good when an outline is memorable. It is not good when the outline is more memorable than the text. And the purpose of the sermon is not to get through the outline. It is to present the message of the text. The outline should be a guide by which you work through the text, not the destination. It is just a means to an end. And you must force it to stay in its place. Don't let it overshadow the text.

SUPPORT THE MAIN IDEA OF THE SERMON

The outline should be more than three things you want to say about the text. It should support the big idea of the message. Once the dominating theme of the text is established, build the outline around it. Undergird the main idea with points that explain, prove, defend, clarify, or apply it. Keep preaching the message of the text as you preach the points of the outline.

PRACTICE UNITY IN YOUR OUTLINE

The movements of the sermon should not be redundant. They should not present the same argument under different headings. Each point should be an independent thought that can stand on its own. But the points of the sermon should not stand so far apart that you cannot see the connection between them. Your outline points should have obvious unity with your main idea and with one another. And the relationship should be clear, obvious, and progressive, moving the message forward to its destination.

KEEP IT MOVING

"Are we there yet?" is a question parents dread to hear during a car trip. Preachers should dread to hear it during sermons, too. Movement will keep the congregation along for the ride. Follow the progression of the text. Let the biblical author's flow of thought lead you. Use the outline to guide the sermon forward. Let your points build on one another. Make it clear that the sermon is going somewhere.

THE SIMPLER THE BETTER

Complicated outlines are distractions. They create a fog in the pulpit that obscures the message. Don't use the outline to impress the congregation or your preaching colleagues. Use it to communicate. And remember that the worst sin of a communicator is to fail to communicate. So avoid terms or concepts in your outline that are confusing. Strive for clarity and simplicity.

MAINTAIN BALANCE

If the points of your outline are points worth making, treat them equally. Don't emphasize one point and use two fillers to complete the outline. Don't spend three minutes on one point and ten minutes on another. Demonstrate that each point of the outline is important by giving them all a fair treatment. If a point is not worth arguing, don't put it into the sermon.

USE SUBPOINTS CAREFULLY

You may have studied the text extensively, but you cannot put all the material you learned into the sermon. Don't create artificial subpoints to stuff the pockets of the sermon with more information. Keep the main thing the main thing in your sermon, and do not let subdivisions of your outline lead you away from the main idea. Only use subpoints if they are natural or necessary, and make sure they are clearly related to the main headings of the outline.

DON'T OVERDO ALLITERATION

If an alliterated outline forms, use it. But do not hunt for words to force alliteration. Use the most natural language in your sermon; few of us speak in alliteration in common conversation. Sure, alliteration can be memorable. But there are other ways to make your outline memorable without alliteration, like asking questions, giving exhortations, and using parallelism.

PUT APPLICATION IN THE OUTLINE

My default mode is to explain the meaning of the text. And I have to work hard to be strategic in application. One simple way I promote application is to put it in the outline. Stick a verb in the outline that calls for action. Write the points as exhortations. Then challenge the congregation to live them out as you explain and illustrate the point.

Chapter 13

CHOOSING
SERMON TITLES

The sermon title is not the most important part of a sermon. And choosing a title is not an essential part of sermon preparation. Understanding the intended meaning of the text and preparing a clear message are infinitely more important than what you title the sermon. Yet selecting compelling sermon titles should not be dismissed as trivial.

Some preachers carelessly slap any title on the sermon after the hard work of preparation. Others decide not to give the sermon a title at all. They just announce a text and plunge right in. This is understandable. It is also unwise. Your sermon needs and deserves a good title. To present a sermon without a title is like trying to sell a book with no title. The most well-respected and well-known authors would not try to do that. Neither should you. There are good reasons for labeling the sermon as clearly and creatively as you can.

- It promotes the content of the sermon.
- It is the first impression the congregation will get of your message.

- It gives the sermon a personal identity.
- It advertises the subject of the sermon beforehand.
- It names the baby before you present it to the world.
- It buys the goodwill of the congregation, as it determines whether to give you their attention.

You should not judge a book by its cover. But people do it anyway. Likewise, you should not judge a sermon by its title. But congregations do it all the time. It does no good to try to fight this reality. Instead, use it for your advantage. Choose a sermon title that reflects the content of your sermon that must be heard. Here are seven practical guidelines for choosing effective sermon titles.

STIMULATE INTEREST

The sermon title advertises the message to grab attention. It is the logo that promotes the biblical message of the text. The title is the sermon concealed. The sermon is the title revealed. Since the title and sermon are so linked, give careful thought to the message's stated name. Craft the title skillfully. Be original. Practice clarity. Use subtlety. Leave mystery. Spark curiosity. Choose a title that holds the congregation's interest until you formally state the proposition of the sermon.

EMPHASIZE SCRIPTURE

Sermon titles may come to you at any time during the preparation process. But it is best to make your final selection after the theme, proposition, and movements of the sermon have been determined. We are to preach the Word, not our sermon title. The text and its message should have priority in the sermon, including the title. So go from text to title, not the other way around. Don't tie the title to a quote or illustration in the sermon. Anchor it to the text. Choose a title that will cause the listener to remember the message of the text.

BE USER-FRIENDLY

The title is not for you. It is for your listeners. So choose a title that is meaningful to the audience. Don't assume they will get obscure theological references. Don't be unnecessarily complex. Don't use technical religious jargon that only you and your systematic theology professor will understand. And don't just slap "Part 2" on last week's sermon title (each sermon should stand on its own, even in a series). Choose a title that will be clear, relevant, and helpful to the congregation.

DON'T OVERPROMISE

The sermon title should accurately represent the text, point, and content of the sermon. The title should not bear false witness against the sermon. It should not make promises the sermon will not fulfill. It should not raise questions the sermon will not answer. It should not announce problems the sermon will not solve. Be honest. Tell the truth. Keep your promise. Make sure the sermon delivers what the title advertises. Guard your pulpit credibility by steering clear of overstatement in the sermon title.

PRACTICE BREVITY

As a general rule, the title should be no more than seven words. "Several Reasons Why the Church Is Not Carrying Out Its Gospel Mission in the World to the Glory of God" is a bad title, for many reasons. Above all, it's way too long. In choosing sermon titles, be succinct. Use an economy of words. Don't try to summarize the entire sermon in the title. However, do not sacrifice clarity for brevity. One-word titles are too broad. You are not really going to preach about "God" or "Love" or "Salvation." You're going to preach a little slice of these great doctrines (e.g., "The Goodness of God," or "The Lord's Command to Love One Another," or "The Way of Salvation"). Choose a specific yet brief title that fits.

AVOID SENSATIONALISM

The title should grab attention, but be careful of sensationalism. The silly can get attention just as easily as the substantial. As Christian preachers, we are royal heralds, not court jesters. We are ambassadors, not clowns. We are called to edify and evangelize, not entertain. Pick a title that piques interest, but do not pick a title for shock value. Do not push the envelope too far. Refuse to use crude, vulgar, flippant, absurd, offensive, irreverent, or ridiculous titles. Always show good taste. Take the preaching assignment seriously. Respect the dignity of the pulpit.

USE VARIETY

Good sermon titles come in different forms. Take advantage of them. Don't be monotonous, especially if you are preaching to the same people every week. Repetitive questions, Scripture quotes, or "how-to" titles soon lose their punch and stereotype your preaching. Stay fresh by trying different title styles.

Consider the following examples:

- Biblical references: "Thorns in the Flesh" or "The Hymn of Christ" or "When You Pray"
- Declarations: "God Knows What He's Doing" or "God Won't Take No for an Answer"

- Questions: "Which Way Are You Going?" or "Are You Faithful?" or "Can You Handle an Answered Prayer?"
- Exclamations: "Trust God!" or "What a Fellowship!" or "Get With the Program!"
- Paradox: "Seeing Is Believing" or "Strength through Meekness" or "The Upside of Down"
- Alliteration: "Practicing the Presence of God" or "Facing Friendly Fire"
- Application: "How to Get to God" or "How to Clean Up Your Life" or "How to Live a Fruitful Life"

Chapter 14

SERMON INTRODUCTIONS

The takeoff is arguably the most important part of a flight. Sprinters work to get a strong start from the blocks to win the race. The opening notes of the song must be right for the song to be performed with excellence. And the introduction is key to preaching a strong message.

The introduction is meant to grab the congregation's attention. Its aim is to build interest and provoke thought. The introduction should make the case for why the listener should actually listen to the rest of the sermon. At the same time, the introduction is just as much for the preacher as it is for the congregation. The congregation will never be interested in a sermon that doesn't seem to be interesting to the preacher. A good introduction should light your fire and stoke your passion for the message of the text.

I typically introduce my sermons in a traditional manner. I read the text first, give the title of the sermon, then formally introduce the message. Others give the introduction before they read the text and state their title. Whichever way you begin your message, a strong introduction is essential, necessary, and beneficial. Here are nine ways to get your sermon off to a good start.

INTRODUCE SOMETHING

Many homileticians encourage preachers to write the introduction last. I am not legalistic about things like this. I think you should write as it comes to you. If the introduction comes to you first, so be it. Yet there is wisdom in not beginning with your introduction. The more you work through the body of the message, the more clarity you will have about how to get into the sermon with a good introduction. Write out a complete sermon skeleton first (as we looked at in chapter 12). Establish the point of the message, organize the structure, and identify objectives of the message. Know what you are introducing before you write your introduction. Then make sure your introduction to the message actually introduces the message.

PLACE THE TEXT IN ITS CONTEXT

A text without a context is a pretext. So make sure to help listeners understand how your text fits into its larger biblical context. Don't drag them through a long survey of the entire book. You are preaching a sermon, not giving a seminary lecture. But help them to see how the text fits into the theme of the section of the book it occurs in, and its relationship with Scripture as a whole. Explain the historical background and literary context, yet avoid the temptation to blitz the congregation with too much exegetical data. Use the introduction to show how your text correlates with the same or similar theme in related Scriptures.

STATE THE POINT OF THE MESSAGE

There is an increasingly popular style of preaching that holds the point of the message until the conclusion. But preachers should view this as a novelty that should not be regularly employed. If you are striving for faithful exposition, find the main point of the text. Craft that point into a clear, direct, one-sentence statement, and state the big idea of the sermon at the beginning. Point to the destination in the introduction. Let the congregation know up front where you are going, even if you don't tell them how you are going to get there.

GIVE AN ACCURATE FORECAST

Some preachers transition from the introduction by summarizing the body of the message that is to come. This is a good practice, even though it can also be good to build suspense by revealing your main ideas as you go. Either way, the introduction should be an accurate forecast of where the sermon is headed. I can't stand it when the weatherperson predicts sunshine and then it rains. However, I understand that the weatherperson only predicts the weather, but doesn't control it. Preachers, on the other hand, can and should ensure that what we forecast in the introduction actually takes place in the message. Don't misrepresent the message. Don't contradict yourself. And don't oversell what you will deliver. If it is not on the shelves, do not put it on the showcase. Present in the introduction what you will proclaim in the message.

WRITE IT OUT

As I've mentioned previously, it is best to write out a complete sermon manuscript, whether or not you use it in the pulpit. But if you do not write out anything else, write out specific sections of the sermon. Your introduction should be one of the sections you write out word for word. You don't want to stumble out of the gate. You want the sermon to begin strong and build momentum as you get to the meat of the message. So untangle your opening thoughts by writing them out. Strive for clarity. Know where you are going. Map your way through the opening moments of the sermon. Establish that the sermon is moving toward a purposeful destination with a clear and compelling introduction.

NO DUMPING ALLOWED

If you take your study seriously, you will inevitably have more material than you can preach in one sermon. What should you do with that additional material? Answer: save it for another message. Do not stick the excess data in the introduction. The introduction is not the place to dump information you cannot find a place for anywhere else. You want your introduction to be clean and tight and strong. Don't undermine it by stuffing it with too much material. The body of the message should be filled with good meat. The introduction should be fat free. So make sure everything in the introduction has a real purpose for being there. Know why every sentence is there, and ruthlessly edit out whatever does not fit.

KNOW YOUR AUDIENCE

Effective preaching requires that you exegete your audience, as well as your text. You should know whom you are preaching to, as well as what you are preaching about. Then craft your introduction for your listeners. Seek to grab the attention of the congregation from the beginning. I admit this is easier if you preach to the same congregation each week. If you are a consistent preacher, your congregation will give you the benefit of the doubt and wait to see where the sermon is going. But don't take them for granted. Keep them on their toes by engaging them in the introduction. If you are preaching in an unfamiliar setting, it is all the more important to make a connection as quickly as possible. Appeal to commonalities, and avoid unnecessary offense. Let the text offend, not your introduction. Plan an introduction that draws them in rather than pushes them away.

PRACTICE VARIETY

Compelling introductions are not easy to develop. Some preachers make their work easier by finding a template to use every time. It simplifies the work, but makes sermons monotonous. Don't start every sermon the same way. Be creative. Use different doors to get into the house. Tell a story. Raise a question. State a problem. Use a strong quote. Make a startling statement. Describe the background of the text. Do an object lesson. Try multimedia. Mix it up. Practice diversity. Change the way you come at them, especially if you preach to the same congregation each week. Practicing variety in the introduction is a simple but effective way to stay fresh in the pulpit.

KEEP IT BRIEF

This is key advice for preachers who strive to do Bible exposition from week to week. You want to spend the bulk of your time explaining and applying the text. So get to the point quickly. Don't ramble. Don't waste words. Don't loiter on the front porch. You can undermine yourself by taking too much time to tell a story, build suspense, or make an application, leaving limited time to deal with the text. Don't saunter through the introduction and then rush through the body of the message. We are prone to say, "I wish I had more time to deal with this." Give yourself more time by keeping your introduction brief. Make the front porch attractive, but don't spend so much time there that the listener does not want to go inside the house. The best things you can show them are inside the text. Get there in a hurry!

Chapter 15

SERMON TRANSITIONS

The preacher prays and reads his text. He states the title of his message. He gives the introduction. He states the point or big idea of the message. Then he prepares to move to the main body of the sermon. He announces his transition to the congregation by saying, "Let me say three things about this text." This is not good. The effective preacher needs to work hard to develop clean, smooth transitional sentences.

Do you know where most car accidents take place? At intersections. Accidents also occur frequently during lane changes. A driver moves from one lane to another without putting on his blinker, which results in a collision. Or a driver assumes that the other drivers will let her over just because she has given a turn signal, which often doesn't happen. Safe drivers use great care in making turns and changing lanes. They are attentive. They put on their signals. They use their mirrors. They look for blind spots. They watch for pedestrians. They drive with the flow of traffic. They wait to be given the right of way. This may seem like a lot of trouble to go through just to change lanes. But it sure beats meeting someone by accident.

Safe drivers make careful transitions. So do good preachers.

You have prayerfully chosen a specific text to preach. You have worked to craft the point of the message in a clear sentence. You have carefully chosen an attention-grabbing title. You have crafted a compelling introduction. You have a powerful message to deliver. Don't weaken the presentation by leaving it up to chance to get you from one place to another in the sermon. Don't stumble into the text by tripping over "three things." Don't get into an accident at the intersection between the first and second point of the sermon because you ran into "things." Don't land the plane awkwardly on the runway of "things."

This is the one piece of advice I want to give you as it relates to using good transitional sentences in preaching. I do not have a list of points to give you in this chapter. I just want to offer one piece of advice: Get "things" out of your sermon. Work hard on your transitional sentences. Move smoothly from one idea to the next. Give a clear signal and get the right of way before you change lanes.

"Things" don't make good transitions. The word "things" is nonspecific. The more specific you are, the more compelling your ideas will be. So try other key words instead of "things."

Give four reasons why believers should pray.

State three requirements for Christian discipleship.

Share five benefits of forgiving people who have wronged you.

Describe the dynamics of a healthy church.

Explain the signs of true conversion.

Present three principles to practice for loving your spouse.

Warn of the dangers of living selfishly.

Get it?

Reasons, requirements, benefits, dynamics, and signs are better than "things." They make transitional sentences concrete, lively, and powerful. There are many effective words you can use to make your transitional sentences come alive. Hunt them down. Practice using them. Work hard to get "things" out of your sermons.

Chapter 16

SERMON ILLUSTRATIONS

There are three basic elements to a sermon: explanation, application, and illustration. At any given point of the sermon, you are doing one of these three things. You are explaining the meaning of the passage. You are exhorting the hearer to live out the truth. Or you are shedding light on the explanation and application of the text through illustration.

Explanation is the foundation of a biblical message. The goal is to explain what the text means by what it says in its context. However, interpretation without application is deficient. You must explain the text and exhort the congregation to do what it says (James 1:22). But your work is not done yet. The effective preacher must also work to clarify meaning, make ideas stick, and call the listener to action.

To this end, illustrations are the preacher's friend. Want proof? Read the Gospels again and note how Jesus taught. The Lord often told parables to illustrate the point of His messages. On many occasions, the parable was the message. Jesus would place some common experience alongside a spiritual truth to reveal and conceal truth at the same time. Yet beyond telling parables, Jesus' teaching was filled with word pictures that helped people see what He was saying. In the same way, a compelling illustration sheds light on the message and helps the congregation see what you are saying. Here are nine tips for making good use of sermon illustrations in your preaching.

ILLUSTRATE!

An illustration that does not illustrate is not an illustration. Worse, it is counterproductive. It actually hurts the sermon. A good illustration is like a window on a house. It helps your listeners see in or out. But merely painting a picture of a window on a wall doesn't help anyone. Giving an illustration just because it's a good story you found and had to tell is counterproductive. Don't just share an anecdote that you think your congregation will find interesting, moving, or entertaining. You are not a comedian going for laughs. You are a herald who has been sent to proclaim a life-changing message. Make sure your illustrations have a relevant point. And remember that you are still obligated to preach the Word as you illustrate.

LOCATION, LOCATION, LOCATION

The value of real estate is based upon its location. The same is true of sermon illustrations. You will hurt the sermon if you stick a story somewhere it does not fit. A story that is too emotional can derail the sermon. People may be moved by it, but they will be moved away from the sermon. You will keep preaching and leave the congregation behind. Position illustrations where they will best clarify the text, highlight the point, or enforce the application. Place the illustration in a strategic place in the sermon. And don't use it at all if it's too good. Illustrations should support the message, not overpower it.

AVOID INDECENT EXPOSURE

The next section of this book will address the importance of being careful about what you reveal about yourself and others in sermon illustrations. But the point should also be made here, in this conversation about illustrations. You must be careful who and what you expose from the pulpit. Get your wife's permission before using your family in the message. Even then, be careful. Don't embarrass people. Only say things that will build people up, not tear them down. Don't reach in the gutter for illustrative material. Tell noble and worthy illustrations. Use parental guidance. Don't say inappropriate things that are unnecessarily offensive. Keep confidential conversations out of the pulpit. And don't be the hero of the stories you tell.

LOOK FOR THEM EVERYWHERE

Life presents possible illustrations every day. Just keep your eyes and ears open, and you will find more illustrations than you can use. People watch. Expect God to point you to a potter's window, as He did with Jeremiah, to rivet a spiritual truth to daily life. And have a means of keeping a record of what you learn. Likewise, if you can get several good ideas from an illustration book, it's worth whatever it costs. Ultimately, Scripture is the best place to find illustrations. Using biblical illustrations allows you to continue to teach as you illustrate. And scriptural illustrations carry divine authority.

WRITE OUT THE ILLUSTRATION

I advocate that preachers write out full sermon manuscripts. But I know this is not always feasible for everyone. To be honest, there are weeks when I have to settle for an extended outline rather than a full manuscript. There are weeks when you just are not able to hammer out a word-for-word document of what you want to say. As a concession, I would advise that you at least write out sections of the sermon. For instance, fully write the introduction and conclusion. Craft your transitional sentences. And write out your illustrations. Make them clear. Include important details. Check your facts. Edit them down. Be creative in writing them out and telling them with style.

DON'T READ THE ILLUSTRATION

If possible, as I've said, write a complete sermon manuscript. But don't read it in the pulpit. Very few preachers are able to communicate effectively by burying their heads in a manuscript and reading a sermon. There needs to be a sense of connection with the congregation. So it helps to prepare a set of notes from the manuscript to use in the pulpit. Again, I understand that some preachers work best with a full script. So here's another concession. Try not to read your illustrations. It is ironic to tell a memorable story but have to read the story rather than share it from memory. Familiarize yourself with the illustration so you can tell it freely in a personal way.

LET THE ILLUSTRATION STAND ON ITS OWN

A good sermon should be able to stand on its own. And so should the illustrations in it. Do not begin the illustration with an apology. If you have to apologize for it, don't tell it. Don't explain the story before you tell it. Don't introduce it by telling the congregation how sad or funny it is. Let them be the judge of that. Comedians say that if you have to explain a joke, it bombed. The same is true with sermon illustrations. If you have to do a detailed exegesis of the sermon illustration, something is wrong. Just give the illustration and let it stand on its own.

DO NOT BEAR FALSE WITNESS!

Tell the truth in your sermon illustrations. Do not bear false witness. Do not make things up and present them as true. Don't stretch the truth to make the story more compelling. You can only stretch the truth so far before it is no longer the truth. An exaggeration is a subtle lie. Consider your sermon illustrations a matter of ministerial ethics. Make sure the story is true. Get the facts straight. Guard your credibility. Be honest and accurate about your sources. Where appropriate, give credit where credit is due. And don't tell someone else's personal story as if it happened to you.

PREACH THE TEXT, NOT THE ILLUSTRATION

We are charged by God to preach the Word (2 Timothy 4:2). The proclamation of Scripture, therefore, must be our priority. So build the sermon around the text, not illustrations. The illustrations should not get more attention than the text. You want the text to speak loud and clear. So give the illustration, make the application, and then move on. Let the text guide the sermon. And don't let a good story lead you astray from your assignment to preach the Word.

Chapter 17

SERMON CONCLUSIONS

"So how was your flight?"

When I am asked this question, I typically respond by saying it was a good flight. I speak positively about the flight for one reason. It landed. I may not like my assigned seat. There may have been no room for my bag in the overhead compartment. It may have been a bumpy flight the whole ride. But none of that matters as long as the flight lands safely. The same is true of sermons. It may get off to a bumpy start. You may have to play catch up to stay within the allotted time schedule. The people on board may not like where the sermon is headed. There may be turbulence the whole time and you never get to a comfortable, cruising altitude to turn off the "Fasten Your Seat Belt" sign. But all will be forgiven if you can safely land the sermon at its intended destination.

Here are seven tips on landing the sermon safely with a strong conclusion.

GIVE A TRUE CONCLUSION

Make sure your conclusion is a true conclusion. Don't just stop the sermon abruptly. Don't let the sermon trail off. Don't preach until you hit your time limit and then sit down. Don't merely go until you run out of material to talk about. Don't simply end by saying a prayer or extending an invitation. Conclude the sermon intentionally. View the sermon as a unit with an introduction, body, and conclusion. And treat the conclusion as important as the other parts of the sermon. Plan out your conclusion. Work to craft a conclusion that is clear, compelling, and climatic.

ONLY CONCLUDE ONCE

We preachers like to note that Paul says "finally" several times in Philippians and then keeps writing. But remember that Philippians is divinely inspired. Our sermons on Philippians are not. So when you say "finally," mean it. If you are not ready to end, don't say it. If you say you are closing the sermon, mean what you say. Don't use the false promise of a conclusion to buy yourself more time. You will only make the congregation nervous if you keep circling the runway. No skilled, responsible pilot plays with the landing gear. And flight attendants don't promise to land early just because the passengers look bored. So don't go into an unnecessary holding pattern by introducing new material at the end. Land when it's time to land.

KNOW YOUR DESTINATION

Where is the sermon going? What is the point of the message? How should the congregation respond to the truth of the text? What are your objectives for the message? What do you want the listener to know, believe, or do? The answers to these questions will determine how to end the message. How can you land the plane safely if you do not know where the runway is? You should take off with a predetermined destination. And the navigational devices of the message should head in that direction and lead to a logical conclusion. A good conclusion is the fitting end of a sermon that has purpose, unity, and movement. Land the message at its intended destination.

REVIEW THE MESSAGE

It is often said that a speaker should tell the audience what he is going to say, then say it, and then tell them what he said. That may be a cliché, but it works. An effective way to conclude a sermon is to review the major points of the message. Don't just repeat the main ideas. Restate them, giving the congregation a look at the same ideas from a different vantage point. Enforce them with solid exhortation. Apply them, showing your people how to live out the life of the teachings of our faith. Illustrate them with good, memorable stories. Celebrate them as reasons to rejoice. Find different ways to drive home the key themes of the message at the end. View the conclusion as the introduction in reverse. Close by making the points again.

ISSUE A CALL TO ACTION

We often separate truth from life, theology from practice, doctrine from duty. But the two are actually inseparable lovers that will not show up without the other. A biblical sermon should both explain and exhort. Application should take place throughout the sermon, but the conclusion is a good place to emphasize it. It is self-deception to hear the Word without doing what it says (James 1:22). It is foolish to look into the mirror of God's Word without making the necessary changes the truth calls for (James 1:23–25). The goal of preaching is application. So end there. Challenge the congregation to live out the teachings of the faith. Exhort them to be doers of the Word. Explain why obedience matters. Show them what following Jesus looks like in practical terms.

RUN TO THE CROSS

Jesus should be the hero of every sermon. The message must be about Him or it is not Christian, biblical preaching. Christ is the good news we proclaim. And the conclusion is a good place to point your hearers to Christ. Of course, the message should be saturated with the gospel. Christ is not honored when He is mentioned at the end of a message that ignores Him throughout. But there is power in concluding with a clear declaration of the gospel. Give a clear explanation of who Christ is and what He has done for us. Run to the cross. Explain the need for salvation and the power of Christ to save. Call the hearer to repent and believe. End by exalting the sufficiency of Christ's divine person and redemptive work.

LEAVE A GOOD IMPRESSION

First impressions are lasting impressions. But so are closing ones. A message that starts with a bang but ends with a whimper loses credibility. A poor conclusion can trump a good introduction and strong main body. It can be like a movie with a good premise that starts strong but seems to run out of material midway through. Good movies carry out the plot to the logical conclusion. The same is true of good sermons. So finish strong. Practice clarity. Use variety. Make it memorable. Strive for an economy of words. Don't ramble. Write it out. Be familiar with it. Think of the conclusion as a lawyer's closing argument. Don't leave any reasonable doubt. Preach for a verdict.

Chapter 18

WRITING SERMON MANUSCRIPTS

The pastor left his sermon manuscript in the pulpit one Sunday. The next morning, the janitor found the manuscript as he was cleaning the sanctuary. And he couldn't resist the urge to read it. The pastor's prepared notes impressed him. He was even moved by what he read, until he stumbled over a note in the margin: "Argument weak here. Start yelling!"

Old story, timeless truth: Passion is never a substitute for clarity. Volume is not a substitute for content. Emotion is not a substitute for conviction. Let me be clear. I have no problem with a preacher yelling sometimes as he is engrossed in the message. But if you write yourself clear, you won't have to yell to cover up a weak argument.

I consider myself a manuscript preacher who cheats. Most weeks, I write a complete manuscript. Most weeks, however, I do not carry anything to the pulpit but my Bible. I typically preach without any notes in front of me. I believe both practices sharpen the preacher —writing manuscripts and preaching without notes. But whether you take notes to the pulpit or not, you should carefully prepare what you want to say and write it out before you stand to preach.

Here are eleven tips for writing yourself clear in sermon preparation.

PRAY

This is not a cursory step. Prayer is crucial to the entire sermon preparation process. You should pray before and throughout your study of the text. And you should pray your way through sermon preparation. You need guidance in what to say and how to say it to your congregation. This is especially true as you work through how you will communicate the Word of God to the people of God. So pray as you write. Pray about your outline, explanation, introduction, illustrations, and applications. Ask God to give you wisdom and the right words to preach Scripture faithfully and clearly.

START WITH A SERMON SKELETON

A sermon skeleton is an overview of the content and structure of the sermon. These are things you should be clear about before you start writing the sermon. You will not have the sermon complete in your mind before you write, but you should have a road map to follow as you work through what you want to say. So begin by determining the title, theme, central idea, outline, and other elements that make up the framework of the message. Establish the structure of the sermon. Then put meat on the bones.

WRITE

You will never write a manuscript if you do not write a manuscript. At some point, you have to put your behind in the seat and write. Don't waste time. Don't procrastinate. Don't make excuses. Sunday is coming. Starting writing. Write for as long as you can. Get your ideas on paper. Don't worry about how good it is yet. This is not the time to edit; it's the time to write. A bad page is better than a blank page. Fill the page now; fix the page later. Just write.

WRITE IT OUT WORD FOR WORD

Type or write out your introduction, explanations of the text, Scripture references, applications, illustrations, transitions, and conclusion. Word for word. "The vacation story" or "Charles Spurgeon quote" or "the movie reference" may suffice in your pulpit notes, but not here. Write it all out. By writing out the vacation story, you get to see how much space it takes up in the sermon. And you have the opportunity to edit it down before you preach it. After you start writing manuscripts regularly, this practice will also help you to gauge how long your sermon is.

WRITE FOR THE EAR

A sermon manuscript is not a term paper, theological essay, or potential book chapter. It is a document containing a message you will deliver to God's people. To be more precise, the manuscript is not a sermon. The preaching of the manuscript is. Preaching is an oral act, not a written one. As you write, think about those who will listen to what you say, not those who may read what you write. When reading, you can stop to ponder the words or look up a word you don't understand. But listeners have to keep listening, or you have lost them. They will check out of the sermon if they do not understand what you are saying. So write for the ear. Speak in plain terms. Avoid unnecessary technical jargon. Use helpful word pictures. Help them to see what you are saying.

PREACH IT AS YOU WRITE IT

Your sermon manuscript will become stronger if you preach it as you write it. Talk it out as you are writing it down. This will help you communicate clearly and effectively. Some words that are easy to write are not easy to pronounce. That long sentence that looks so beautiful on your computer screen may be a nightmare to say or hear. And sometimes you cannot tell that an idea does not make sense until you hear the words come out of your mouth. But talking your way through the sermon as you write it will aid clarity. Preaching it as you write it also aids memorization.

STRIVE FOR CLARITY

Process your word choices, sentence structures, cross-references, transitional sentences, and illustrations as clearly as possible. If you do, style and creativity will take care of themselves. Clarity is its own virtue.

CRAFT TRANSITIONAL SENTENCES

It bears repeating that car accidents often happen at intersections and during lane changes. Likewise, moving from the introduction to the main body, from point 1 to point 2, or from illustration to application can be as dangerous as driving in rush hour traffic. So work on smooth transitions. Don't just say, "Let me say three things about the text." Give them three reasons to pray or four ways to resist temptation or two benefits of trusting God. Let your transitions be smooth and specific so that your audience can follow your train of thought.

WORK AROUND WRITER'S BLOCK

I rarely write a sermon from beginning to end. I first struggle to write my introduction and conclusion. Inevitably, I will continue to struggle to get my thoughts out as I move from point to point. This used to hinder me from getting my work done. But I have found a simple way to work around writer's block. I simply write as it comes to me, whichever part of the sermon it is. If the second point is clear in my mind before the first point, I start there. If the conclusion comes to me before the introduction, so be it. If I get a mental block at a particular juncture, I start working on another part of the sermon. This helps me to keep writing when a section is not yet clear, and it keeps me moving forward to get my work done.

MARK THE MANUSCRIPT FOR PREACHING

I do not plan to take my manuscript to the pulpit. But I write as if I will. I mark up the manuscript so that the different parts of the sermon will jump out at me. I put the main points in red font, subpoints in dark blue. Scripture references are italicized. Quotes are blue. Illustrations are purple. "Runs" are green. Hymn lyrics are orange. I highlight, underline, and change font sizes. These markings keep me from being a slave to the manuscript if I happen to take it to the pulpit. The various sections pop out on the page so that I can preach more easily from section to section, rather than word for word. Likewise, this process helps me absorb the message into my memory.

EDIT RUTHLESSLY

The manuscript is a draft until you preach it. Keep working on it until then. Don't fall in love with the document. Consider it a work in progress that continually needs updating. Explain technical words or choose simpler ones. Shorten your sentences. Take out cliché or overused words and phrases. Find a different way to say it to keep things interesting. Use one cross-reference instead of three.

Cut out that section that was good study material but doesn't fit in the message. Eliminate unnecessary repetition. Have the courage to leave some hard work on the cutting room floor for the sake of clarity, unity, and movement.

Chapter 19

PREACHING
WITHOUT NOTES

We were hanging out at the church, when a woman I had never met before pulled up, parked, and since she didn't know me, walked right past me on her way into the building. She was there to pick me up for the service I was scheduled to preach at her church that afternoon. My father had told her pastor I would preach their youth service. But he forgot to tell me! So there I was. On my way to preach. Barely in my teens. Scared out of my wits. I preached the story of David and Goliath. It was a Scripture I knew, and it was a message I had recently preached. But I did not know how I would get through without my manuscript.

I learned two things from this experience. First of all, I began to take seriously the advice I had heard my father give preachers many times: Always be ready! Keep a message in your head, your heart, and your pocket. I likewise discovered that day that I could preach without notes. It was a baptism by fire. More than twenty-five years later, I am used to preaching without notes. I still write sermon manuscripts, but I rarely use them in the pulpit. If I need the manuscript, an extended outline, or an index card of notes, so be it. I will not sacrifice content for style. But most weeks, if I have done my work in the study, I don't need anything but a Bible when I stand to preach.

Each person has to decide if preaching without notes is right for them. It may not be for you, and that's okay. Some of the best preachers of our day use full manuscripts in the pulpit, and it does not hurt their preaching in the least. For that matter, most of the preachers I know personally preach with notes. Very few go to the pulpit without the safety net of sermon notes. You must determine what is best for you. Don't try to go to battle wearing Saul's armor. Go to the pulpit with your slingshot and five smooth stones.

Do you want to preach without notes? Here are eleven practical recommendations that will help you learn to preach without notes.

START GRADUALLY

If you want to preach without notes, do not transition from using a full manuscript to note-free preaching right off the bat. Whittle your manuscript down to a page or two. Start with limited notes. Use just an extended outline. Take baby steps. As your confidence grows, try preaching without a safety net.

GET AN EARLY START

As I've said a few times by now, start your sermon preparation as early as possible. Saturday-night specials undermine effective preaching without notes. Last-minute study will rob you of clarity, creativity, and confidence. The more time you spend with the text, the more it will benefit your preparation and presentation. So don't procrastinate. Start as early in the week as you can. Give your peak hours to study. And stay in the seat until the hard work is done.

MASTER THE TEXT

Study the text diligently. A key way to have greater freedom in the pulpit is to enslave yourself to the text in the study process. Work hard to make sure you understand the meaning and message of the text. If you sweat in the study, you can relax in the pulpit. You may not remember every quote, reference, or list, but you can preach with confidence when you know the meaning and message of the text. Do a good job in the study. Then stand and explain, apply, and illustrate what you have learned.

CRAFT A SERMON SKELETON

Create a clear sermon skeleton. An essential key to preaching without notes is to have a clear structure for your sermon. Call it an outline, movements, or whatever. You need to know where this sermon is going. And you need to know how you plan to get there. A clear path produces smooth preaching.

WRITE IT OUT

Write a full manuscript. Preaching without notes is not an excuse for pulpit sloth. It is not a license to preach extemporaneously. You should write a full manuscript, even though you don't plan to use it in the pulpit. The process of thinking through what you want to say and how you want to say it will help you preach clearly and confidently without notes.

BE CLEAR

Make clarity the top priority. You will find note-free preaching to be more difficult if your goal is to be cute or clever. Don't stuff your sermon with filler material. Stick to the basics. Don't try to be impressive. Work to prepare a message that your congregation will understand, not one that will impress your seminary professors.

TAKE IT IN

Internalize the material. You are not cramming for a test. You are preparing to deliver a message. Read the sermon through several times. Mark up the manuscript. Think through your transitions. Sing the hymn you plan to quote. Pray over the sermon. Examine yourself in light of what you will be preaching to others. Work to get it in your heart, not just your head.

USE WORD ASSOCIATIONS

Master the material through word associations. I use word associations to memorize my sermons. If I can remember key words, I'm ready. For instance, I may use six words to remember my introduction: Quotation, Context, Text, Point, and Transitional Sentence. These words tell me to start with the quote, address the historical background, land at the text, state the point of the message, and then transition to the outline. I can work through the first page of a manuscript by memorizing these word associations.

REHEARSE THE MATERIAL

Practice the message. I trust you are beyond standing in the mirror to rehearse your sermon. But you should preach it aloud. As you exercise. In the car. While you are dressing. Use every opportunity to talk through the message. There is something about hearing yourself say the words that aids memorization. It works. Try it. But warn your family first, so they won't think you are going crazy.

BE FLEXIBLE

Preach the message, not the manuscript. If you do not get to say everything you prepared, so what? The One who guides the preparation of the message governs the presentation of it. And He has the right to edit your sermon as you preach it! Your job is to preach the message the Lord gives you as He leads you, not to say everything you wrote in the manuscript.

DIVE IN

Just do it. You will not learn to preach without notes if you never preach without notes. At some point, you must suck it up, face your fears, and trust God to help you preach what He has taught you in private. It is a step of faith, for sure. But God is faithful. Trust Him to help you preach without notes. Then just do it!

Part 3:

POINTS OF WISDOM FOR PREACHING

Chapter 20

BEING YOURSELF
IN THE PULPIT

My father let me preach for him during one of our 8:00 a.m. worship services. I was fourteen, maybe fifteen. I worked hard on the sermon, as hard as a fourteen-year-old preacher can work on a sermon. But I took the opportunity seriously and gave it my best. By that I mean my sermon was a collage of the best of my favorite preachers. I was like the image in Nebuchadnezzar's dream (Daniel 2). I was a little bit H. B. Charles Sr., a little Jasper Williams, and a little bit C. A. W. Clark. And I definitely had clay feet.

As I sat down from preaching, however, no one could have told me that I did not just preach a great sermon. My father stood up and did just that. He was supposed to be giving pastoral remarks to the congregation before the offering. He started talking about me, instead. I remember it like it was yesterday. "Pray for me, church," he said, shaking his head. "I have a long way to go with my son. He's not going to go far," Dad continued, "until he recognizes that there are many other preachers that can beat him being Jasper Williams, Donald Parsons, and Caesar Clark. But no one can beat him being H. B. Charles Jr."

I heard what he said that day. But I wasn't listening to him. I didn't see anything wrong with what I had done. I was convinced that imitating was the way to success in ministry. But I was confronted by the error of my ways not too long after my father's death.

I had been invited to preach at a local district association meeting. It was a great honor for such a young preacher. I wanted to be my best. So I stole a sermon from one of my favorite preachers. Not only did I preach his sermon, but I tried to imitate his voice, style, and mannerisms as I preached. I just knew that the audience would be impressed with how well this young man could preach!

But one older pastor who was present was obviously not impressed. He was sitting on the platform, and as I was preaching, his bold voice yelled out, "Say it, Jasper!" I thought I was hearing things. I had to be. But then he said it again. "Say it, Jasper." A few minutes later, "Preach, Jasper!" I guess I wasn't the only one who had heard Jasper Williams preach that sermon.

"He is so wrong for doing this," I angrily thought to myself as I limped to the end of the sermon. In all actuality, he was right. H. B. Charles Jr. was the announced preacher for the occasion. But it was Jasper Williams who stood up to preach that night. A very poor imitation of Jasper Williams. Whoever it was standing behind the pulpit that night, it wasn't H. B. Charles Jr. And it definitely wasn't Jasper Williams. It was some strange pulpit chameleon who deserved to be mocked. When the whole sad ordeal was over, I could hear my father saying, "H. B. is not going to get far until he recognizes that no one can beat him being H. B. Charles Jr."

It is said that imitation is the best form of compliment. But this is not true in the pulpit. If preaching is truth through personality, to proclaim the truth dressed up as some other personality is not to preach. It is pulpit identity theft. No preacher is completely original.

We are all influenced by other preachers. We are shaped by our teachers. We are reflections of our pulpit heroes. It's inevitable. But it should not be intentional.

God has called *you*. God has gifted *you*. God has prepared *you*. God has given *you* an assignment. God has given *you* a message to proclaim. The Lord made you an original. Don't settle for being a cheap copy of someone else. No one can beat you being you.

Chapter 21

DEVELOPING YOUR STYLE OF PREACHING

I am sometimes asked how I developed my style of preaching. This question is somewhat amusing because it assumes I have an intentionally developed style of preaching. That is giving me way too much credit. Like most pastors, I just do what I do every week. The challenge of weekly preparation, along with other personal and pastoral duties, leaves little time for exploring different styles of preaching. But after years of preaching weekly, certain characteristics have formed in my pulpit ministry. Yet I believe there are ways you can establish your own voice in preaching. These are not revolutionary ideas. They are simple, basic principles to practice in order to grow in your pulpit ministry and develop your own "style" of preaching.

PREACH

The preaching task is caught as much as it is taught. You learn to preach by preaching. Of course, experience alone will not make you a better preacher if you don't learn from mistakes or practice fundamental principles (many of which are found in the preceding chapters). You will only continue to make the same mistakes in the pulpit over and over again. But experience combined with an openness to learning cultivates stronger preaching. So take advantage of every opportunity to teach and preach—worship services, Sunday school classes, prayer meetings, or any other setting where you get to open the Word to teach. And take every preaching assignment seriously. Pray and prepare diligently, and give the Lord all you've got. Preach as if it is the first time, may be the best time, and could be the last time. As you preach, you are stirring up the gift that is in you. And each experience becomes a lesson from which you can learn and grow.

STUDY PREACHING

Good preaching is not just an art. It is also a science. There are rules to obey, guidelines to follow, and principles to practice for effective preaching. So one of the best things you can do is study preaching. Become a student of homiletics. Work to master your craft. Read at least one substantial book on preaching each year. Go back to school, if you can. Take advantage of ongoing learning opportunities like conferences and similar events. Learn, follow, and master the rules. Then, eventually, you will be good enough to break them.

FOCUS ON THE MESSAGE

Second Timothy 4:2 says, "Preach the word." Paul exhorts Timothy to preach, to be a herald for the King. He also explains what Timothy is to preach: the Word. It is the content of our preaching that makes us faithful, not the style. Style does not matter if you mishandle the Word. Your style should serve the message. Let your style develop around what you have to say, not the other way around. If you focus on style at the expense of the message, you are an entertainer, not a preacher. Getting the message right is the primary thing. The Lord will hold you responsible for how you handle the message. He won't care about how good your style is. So keep your priorities straight.

BE YOURSELF

Preachers inevitably learn to preach by listening to other preachers. Even if we receive formal training, we are still shaped by the preaching that we hear, not just the theory that we study. We are all influenced by preaching voices in our heads. To this day, I have to limit how much I listen to my favorite preachers, lest I carry them into the pulpit with me on Sunday morning. I want to be a voice, not an echo. Preaching is truth through personality. So be yourself. The congregation will forgive you for not being Dr. so-and-so. They will not forgive you for not being you!

EXPOSE YOURSELF TO GREAT PREACHING

I pity the congregation that only hears one preacher. And I pity the preacher who only listens to one preacher, especially if he is that one preacher! Sitting under the ministry of others will feed your faith and elevate your preaching. Read classic sermons by other preachers. Listen to sermons by noted preachers. Hear respected preachers in person, when you have the opportunity. Expose yourself to great preaching. The more, the better. Following various effective preachers will help you resist the urge to mimic any particular preacher. It is often said that there are two times a preacher wants to preach—when he hears a preacher who can preach well, and when he hears one who cannot. In listening to others, you will either learn what to do or what not to do. But it is important that you listen to preaching as a student as well as a sinner.

PRACTICE SELF-CRITIQUE

Most preachers hate to listen to themselves, unless they are on an ego trip. Recordings of our messages are never as good as we thought the sermon was when we preached it. So we are prone to avoid the torture of listening to ourselves. But force yourself to listen to your sermons. If you can watch them, that's even better. Make note of bad habits, sloppy speech, and distracting patterns. Don't be narcissistic about this. And don't try to whitewash your preaching of idiosyncrasies that reflect who you are. But examine where there is room for improvement and take steps.

GET HEALTHY FEEDBACK

All of us have blind spots we cannot see. Be willing to receive constructive criticism and legitimate encouragement. It's hard. But it's worth it. Seek feedback from your wife. She loves you and has your best interests at heart. And she knows you the best. So talk to her about your sermons. Just don't do it on Sunday afternoon! Likewise, ask family and friends where you can improve. Talk to your staff or associate ministers. Consult people who listen to you regularly to get their advice. They will have a better feel for what is typical or an exception in your preaching. Then get feedback from someone who does not sit under your preaching every week. Let someone with fresh eyes point out what you may not see. Don't give critics opportunities to abuse you, but seek out sincere people who will help you grow in your preaching through healthy feedback.

STRIVE FOR EXCELLENCE

I have a confession: I want to be a great preacher. Don't get me wrong. I am not trying to be viewed as great in the eyes of men. But I do want to be the best preacher I can be for God. I want to fulfill my ministry. I want to be a faithful herald for the King. Desire to be the best preacher you can be for God. Don't compete with other preachers. Compete against the preacher you are now. Labor hard to be a better preacher a year from now than you are today. Determine to never stop growing. Don't be content with where you are. Work to be a prepared, strong, and growing minister. Let your progress be evident to all (1 Timothy 4:15).

BE PATIENT

My preaching has developed naturally as I grow older and more mature. There are things I said and did years ago that do not fit me anymore. The passing of time has a way of shaping your preaching. I sometimes go back to a sermon that I preached ten years ago. The exegesis can be sound, but I still cannot just put it in the microwave and preach it again. I must work hard to update the message to reflect where I am now in my spiritual maturity and ministerial development. I am a work in process, as are you. So be careful of defending the way you preach now. You may grow out of it by this time next year. Give yourself room to grow.

DON'T WORRY ABOUT IT

As you exercise your gifts, your preaching will develop on its own. And it will be a natural formation, rather than a synthetic product. If you are too concerned about matters of style, it will handicap your preaching. I cannot say this enough. Preaching is not about the preacher. It is about the royal message that we preach. You will have a car accident if you are preoccupied with what you see in the vanity mirror. Pay attention to the road. Stay in your lane. Focus on getting to your final destination.

Chapter 22

PULPIT CONSISTENCY

There was a pastor I listened to regularly during the early days of my ministry. I really enjoyed his preaching. He ministered to me. And I would joyfully commend him to other preachers. This pastor was not well known to many of the preachers I talked to. And they would inevitably ask me what his preaching was like.

"He can say it," I would respond, "if you catch him at the right time."

A friend gave me a lot of tapes of this pastor over the years. Some of the messages were stellar examples of Bible exposition. It was some of the best preaching I had heard. Other times, not so much. When he was good he was really good. And when he was bad he was really bad. He sometimes used the text to make a point the text was not actually saying. Other times he would preach questionable charismatic teachings. On one tape, he admitted to making false prophecies in the past. At that point, I asked my friend not to give me any more tapes of this pastor. I couldn't take it anymore.

When this preacher decided to preach the text, it was exceptional. If you caught him right, he could preach with the best of them. I didn't see any problem with this qualification I would make when commending his preaching, because it was honest. Until someone asked an obvious but stunning question: "What if you don't catch him right?"

This question hit me squarely on the chin. And I did not know how to respond. Ultimately, I stopped commending this pastor. I changed my view of good preaching. And I started to check myself and the consistency of my pulpit work.

I don't want people to have to catch me right. This has nothing to do with how clever the message is. It has nothing to do with how smooth my presentation may be. And it has nothing to do with how the congregation responds. It has everything to do with how I handle the Word of truth. I want to get it right every time I stand to preach.

A faithful preacher must be consistent. Every sermon does not have to be a home run. Every sermon will not be a home run. But you can make sure you get on base each week. That should be your goal. Don't strive to preach great sermons. Strive to preach consistently good sermons. And, every now and then, one will be great.

Aim to be consistent. It is not enough to get it right now and then. Who cares if you know how to preach the Word if you choose not to for whatever reason? That's treason. It's prostitution. It's just plain wrong. There's a word for a man who is only faithful to his wife when you catch him right: *unfaithful*!

The congregation should not have to catch us right for us to faithfully preach the Scriptures. If we do not have the text right, we should not get in the pulpit until we do. Get the text right or don't preach it. And do not compromise once you get into the pulpit. The crowd, event, or atmosphere must not be an excuse to compromise your charge to preach the Word. Paul testified, "And I, when I came to you, brothers, did not come proclaiming to you the testimony of God with lofty speech or wisdom. For I decided to know nothing among you except Jesus Christ and him crucified. And I was with you in weakness and in fear and much trembling, and my speech and my message were not in plausible words of wisdom, but in demonstration of the Spirit and of power, so that your faith might not rest in the wisdom of men but in the power of God" (1 Corinthians 2:1–5).

There may be times when the preacher does not catch the congregation right. After all, preaching is out of season at some times and in some places. Some churches will not endure sound doctrine that rebukes, reproves, and exhorts with complete patience and teaching. Some people would rather hear an ear-tickler than a gospel herald. There are congregations that want the preacher to make them feel good rather than to tell them the truth. But it should never be said that you failed to rightly represent the Word to your congregation.

Your people should not wonder what they are going to get from you from week to week. Strive to be as clear, compelling, and creative as you can. By all means, don't bore people with the gospel. But do not be creative in the pulpit at the expense of the truth. Sure, you shouldn't have to choose between truth and passion. But if I had to choose, I would rather my pastor's preaching be faithful though boring, rather than stirring but misleading. Needing a Red Bull before church is better than needing a spiritual antidote to save you from doctrinal poison after church! Don't be a preaching chameleon. Don't be Reverend Jekyll and Pastor Hyde.

Be consistent. Be faithful. Be right whenever they catch you.

Chapter 23

INDECENT EXPOSURE
IN THE PULPIT

To illustrate is to shed light on a subject. It is to help the listener see with the ear. Illustrations are like windows in a house. They let the light in. But they can also let in voyeurs, seeking to glimpse the forbidden. This is why most windows have curtains, blinds, or shades. But voyeurism can be facilitated by those who want to show what they should not show. There is no place for promoting voyeurism in the pulpit. Sermon illustrations should be like letting sunlight into a window, not like putting a spotlight on a stage. You must be careful to guard the dignity of the pulpit. Here are ten guidelines for avoiding indecent exposure in preaching.

THOU SHALT NOT EMBARRASS THY NEIGHBOR

When I got married, my wife, Crystal, gave me blanket permission to use anything from our life together I thought would be appropriate or helpful in my preaching. But she had one qualification: "Don't embarass me." She said it softly, but the expression of her face virtually screamed at me. I got the point. I respected her concern. And she has never had to issue that warning again. I strive to keep this important commandment: "Thou shalt not embarrass thy neighbor." And so should you. Don't say anything that will embarrass your family and friends. For that matter, don't embarrass your enemies, either. Don't criticize, settle scores, or take shots from the pulpit. Affirm, don't embarrass.

THINK TWICE

Extemporaneous preaching can be dangerous. Many inappropriate things are said spontaneously in the midst of preaching. We just don't think about it before we say it. This is another reason you should write out your messages completely. A full manuscript gives you the opportunity to test ideas in the lab before you say them in public. And as much as you can, stick to the script. If you stray from what you prepared, and it includes a personal reference you have not thought through, think twice. And because you may not have time to think through it on your feet, it's better not to say it.

DO NOT BOAST

Arrogant boasting is evil (James 4:16). No Christian should ever be found boasting in himself, especially a minister of Jesus Christ. Has the Lord blessed you generously? Praise Him. But do not brag about it in the pulpit. Are you in a season where your church is doing well? Wonderful. But don't talk about it in the pulpit like you are some shrewd and successful CEO. You should not use illustrations about what you drive, where you live, what designers you wear, how much money you have, who you know, or anything else that conveys that you have it going on. Don't use the pulpit to brag about material things. Don't use the pulpit to brag about your ministry accomplishments. Don't use the pulpit to brag on yourself.

ASK PERMISSION

A simple way to stay out of trouble is to ask permission before you mention someone from the pulpit. If you are not sure the person you are mentioning will be comfortable with it, ask. If you think a reference may be too sensitive, ask. If you think what you share may cause a negative reaction, ask. Get permission first and you won't have to get forgiveness later. Ask to share the story.

DO NOT USE ILLUSTRATIONS
FROM COUNSELING SESSIONS

In many instances, church members do not confide in their pastors or other members because they fear their private business will be broadcast from the pulpit. "Please don't talk about me from the pulpit," they plead. They may say it with a smile. But they mean it. Your people should trust that their discussions with you are confidential. Of course, you cannot promise absolute confidentiality. There are certain sins and struggles that we may be spiritually or legally required to disclose. But those issues will need to be shared with specific persons or authorities, not the congregation. You undermine this confidence when you use counseling conversations as pulpit material.

SPARE US THE DETAILS

Once or twice a year, I permit unplanned testimonies in worship. I think it is good and healthy for the congregation to hear how the Lord is at work in the lives of the saints (Psalm 107:2). But I first remind volunteers that they cannot tell it all. It just seems the more details they try to give, the more the testimony goes astray. The same thing happens in preaching. The more details about a situation, conversation, or experience you give, chances are you will overspeak or exaggerate. As Solomon pointed out, "Whoever restrains his lips is prudent" (Proverbs 10:19). So only say what is necessary to get your point across.

DON'T PLAY THE HERO

Avoid illustrations in which you are the star. You don't want people to think more highly of you than they ought. A surefire way to produce misguided hero worship is to tell stories that feature you as the hero—the one who prayed or forgave or sacrificed or exhibited patience or led someone to Christ. For every story of answered prayer, there is a story of a failure to pray. For every story of winning a lost person to Christ, there is a story of resisting the Spirit's urging to be a witness for Christ. Don't magnify yourself. Let Jesus be the hero.

GOOD FOR THE SOUL, BAD FOR THE REPUTATION

If there is something you need to confess, tell it to the Lord—not to your congregation! Beware that in the attempt to prove that you are human, you can give the indication that you are not spiritually qualified to preach. Even if it is something that is buried in the past of your pre-Christian days, still be careful. Paul says that it is shameful to speak of those things that are done in the dark (Ephesians 5:12). You want to invite prodigals home, not make the far country seem desirable.

MAKE SURE YOU ARE OVER
IT BEFORE YOU TALK ABOUT IT

When we have gone through hurts and pains and sorrows, we want to share the lessons we have learned with our people. Indeed, others can benefit from the things the Lord has brought you through. But make sure you are through it before you talk about it publicly. Let the lessons you've learned sit a while. Make sure you first pass the class before sharing your notes. Don't bring up subjects that you are not spiritually or emotionally ready to share. The worship service is not group therapy. Don't regurgitate your hurt feelings, open wounds, or unhealed offenses onto your congregation.

REMEMBER IT'S NOT ABOUT YOU

The best way to avoid indecent exposure in the pulpit is to stay focused on the fact that the message is not about you. And it is not about your people, either. It is about the Lord Jesus Christ. Your people should learn more about Christ from your sermons than they learn about you. "For what we proclaim is not ourselves," said the apostle Paul, "but Jesus Christ as Lord, with ourselves as your servants for Jesus' sake" (2 Corinthians 4:5).

Chapter 24

PULPIT
PLAGIARISM

I stood to preach, called my text, and confidently began speaking the message that was on my heart. But there was a weird response. Something strange was happening in the room, but I didn't know what it was. I couldn't catch the vibe. I had preached this event for the past several years. Many people in the congregation had heard me preach before. I knew what to expect from them. And they knew what to expect from me. Yet the congregation was unsettled throughout the entire message. But I couldn't figure out why.

After I sat down, it all became clear.

The pastor sitting next to me leaned over and told me the speaker who had opened the meeting several nights before had preached the same text and a similar message. For some reason, this news made me nervous. Yet I was at peace at the same time. I had preached what I believed the Lord wanted me to say that night. And my message was the result of my Bible study and sermon preparation. It was my message, and my original material. It was the product of my own labor over the text.

After the service, my host gave me a copy of the other pastor's message. When I got to my hotel room, I crawled into bed with my computer and listened to it from start to finish. Indeed, it was the same text. And it was in many respects similar to my message. We both preached the same doctrinal theme from the text. But we organized the messages differently and labeled our points differently. I worked through the message with three main points in my outline. He had four. The homiletical approach was different as well. And the way we argued the message was different, though we were preaching on the same doctrine.

The whole strange experience got me thinking about the ethical matter of pulpit plagiarism.

Vance Havner used to say that when he began preaching, he was determined to be original or nothing. "I ended up being both," he quipped. Yet all faithful preachers deliver an unoriginal, "stolen" message—the Word of God. Biblical preaching exposes the authorial intent of the text: the divine message the human writer was moved to communicate. It is God's message. We are only heralds of the God-breathed message of Scripture.

If we read the text right, what we see will be pretty close to the conclusions drawn by other faithful Bible expositors. That ought to be the case, at least. If you come up with a reading of the text that no one else has ever thought of in the history of the church, you're wrong! Most Bible expositors use many of the same exegetical resources. We drink from the same fountains. We dig in the same fields. So it should be no surprise for you to hear two messages that "overlap," for lack of a better term. But let's be clear. Stealing other people's material and preaching it as if it is your own work is wrong.

After the tragic shootings at Virginia Tech in 2007, a certain pastor preached a message he claimed the Lord had given him. Later that week, his local newspaper outed him, revealing the message was actually from a website that sells sermons. This "inspired" message had, in fact, been preached and posted by several other pastors across the country that same day! This is wrong. The eighth commandment should apply to our pulpit work: "You shall not steal" (Exodus 20:15). I am not saying that you shouldn't use sources. On the contrary, there is wisdom in the multitude of counselors (Proverbs 15:22). And it is arrogant for you to study a text and preach a sermon on it without consulting the wisdom of those who have in some instances spent a lifetime studying these passages, books, or themes.

When you do the hard work of personal study and sermon preparation, something wonderful can happen. For instance, you can stand and preach a text that was just preached in that same pulpit three days earlier, and you can make the same point the previous sermon made. Yet God can use your preaching—*your* preaching!—to declare the unchanging truth of God's Word in a fresh, new, and life-changing way.

That's my two cents on pulpit plagiarism.

Now let me take one cent back.

Indeed, a man should do his own homework and come to the pulpit with the fruit of his own study. However, I repeat, no one is original. And no preacher should try to be. When we stand to preach or teach the Word, it should be our primary goal to be faithful and clear. Brothers, the Lord does not ask us to be cute, clever, or creative in our ministry of the Word. This is not an excuse to bore people with the gospel. But our preaching should exalt the Lord Jesus Christ, not our pulpit brilliance. It's a seesaw, and you cannot exalt both Christ and yourself at the same time. So we should not try so hard to have our own "voice" that the congregation is not able to encounter Christ as they listen to the sermon.

We live in a time when there are so many helpful resources available that no one has an excuse for not being prepared. And we must not be so proud, foolish, or shortsighted that we refuse to accept help. Over the years, I have benefited greatly from pastors who are generous with their sermon material. And it has brought me to a place where I am not very possessive about my work. I try to share my material as freely as I can. My philosophy is that if I write or say something that can help you in your presentation of the Word, feel free to use it. Extract from it what works for your message or congregation. If some of my bullets fit your gun, load up and shoot.

My work has my fingerprints on it, which includes both my strengths and weaknesses. If someone is going to use my material effectively, he must edit it heavily to determine what works best for him. But if you find it easy to use my material, I take it as a compliment. It means my work is "portable." And I am glad to help. Sunday's coming! And the burden of weekly preparation is so difficult that we should seek to help one another in any way we can. And we should look for help from wherever we can find it.

Bottom line: Milk a lot of cows. But churn your own butter.

Chapter 25

PROTECTING YOUR VOICE FOR PREACHING

A new friend sent me a text. "Do you have any advice for voice control in and out of the pulpit?" he asked.

I don't really take care of my voice as I should, even though it does not take much for me to lose my voice. And during the preaching moment, managing rate, pitch, and volume often leaves me out of gas by the end of the sermon. So I'm not an expert on this subject by any means. Yet I ventured a brief answer for my friend. This chapter is my fuller answer to his question.

My father had a big, strong preaching voice. And many of my early preaching heroes sounded like preachers, whatever that means. I do not have a preacher's voice. But I tried to sound big. Unfortunately, it sounded like Simba practicing his roar in *The Lion King*. This resulted in me often losing my voice in preaching. I had to learn ways to protect my voice in and out of the pulpit. Over the years, these simple practices have helped me to maintain my voice for preaching.

GET SOME REST

Nothing saves your voice for preaching like resting it before you preach. But it is often hard for me to sleep on Saturday nights. As a result, there are many Sunday mornings that I give the Lord a ready mind and heart, but a tired body. One of the best things you can do for your preaching overall is go to sleep on Saturday. Or take a nap before you preach an evening service. Rest your voice. Don't spend a lot of time talking before you preach. If you can avoid it, don't lead every part of the service in which you are preaching. Make sure your instrument is ready when it matters the most.

DRINK PLENTY OF WATER

This may be the only good habit in my diet. I drink a lot of water, especially before I preach. I also try to avoid drinking milk or colas. Just water. I even keep a glass of water on the pulpit at my home church, just in case. Most weeks I don't need it. But I would rather have it and not need it than to need it and not have it. If my voice begins to get dry or scratchy, I will pause to drink a sip of water. But it must be room temperature water for me. If I drink cold water before I speak, it will close up my voice.

AVOID EXOTIC VOCAL CURES

I have known preachers who drank ice-cold colas before they preached. I have also known preachers who drink piping hot tea or coffee before preaching. Many other preachers drink special concoctions beforehand to clear their voices. To each his own. For me, rest and water seem to be good enough. And I would advise you to avoid becoming dependent upon special remedies. A guest pastor drank a special potion before he preached for me many years ago.

A few weeks later, my voice was sore between services. The ushers made me some of that potion. I stood in the pulpit looking troubled. One of the preachers asked if something was wrong. I mumbled, "I cannot feel my lips or my tongue!" That was the last time I used that potion.

GET GOOD MONITORS

Having floor monitors on the platform that will project your voice back to you is quite helpful in protecting the voice of the preacher. If I cannot hear myself, I start talking louder and preaching harder. I assume the congregation cannot hear me, because I can't hear myself. Unfortunately, there are many days when my presentation is shaped by the fact that I cannot hear myself. If you are a pastor, make sure you have good monitors. Make sure you have people on the soundboard who know what they are doing! Consider the sound guy your best friend when you have to preach.

PACE YOUR PRESENTATION

In this regard, voice lessons, speech training, or presentation feedback can be valuable to the preacher. You need to learn how to pace yourself in the presentation. Talk at a comfortable pace. Use pauses. Raise your voice for emphasis. At other times, whisper. Speak at a pitch that's comfortable for you.

I was preaching at a convention. In my nervousness, I started preaching in a high voice. I was thinking to myself, "What are you doing?" But I couldn't stop. Halfway through the sermon, I had no voice. The same will happen to you if you do not pace yourself. Take your time. Don't be in a hurry. The sermon is a marathon, not a sprint. You don't want to run out of gas at point two. Pace yourself.

GUARD YOUR INSTRUMENT

Some singers wear hats and scarves even on warm, sunny days, determined to protect their voices. You do not have to go to extremes. But protect your instrument. Wear a coat when necessary. Don't ride to the service with the air in the car directly on you. Refuse to sit under AC vents in the service. Do what it takes to guard your voice. But do not be neurotic about these things. Just be careful that you are not carelessly doing things that will rob you of your strength to preach.

DO YOUR HOMEWORK

I am always nervous when I stand up to preach. However, after the first minutes of the sermon, I am able to calm down. It is the ministering help of the Holy Spirit that enables me to relax and preach. It is also the assurance that I have done my homework. I know what I want to say and, most of the time, how I want to say it. This eases tension and removes anxieties that can affect your voice as you preach.

DON'T WORRY ABOUT IT

As a young preacher, I had the opportunity to quiz one of my favorite preachers. I asked him what he did to protect his voice. Firmly but graciously, he responded that young preachers like me worry about stuff like that. He claimed that he did not worry about it anymore. He just got up with whatever he had in the way of voice and preached the message God had given him. I thought his answer was ridiculous. But now as an older preacher, I fully agree. Focus more on the message than the delivery. And trust that God will give you what you need to be faithful to your assignment (2 Corinthians 12:7–10).

Chapter 26

BEING A
GUEST PREACHER

I am a local church pastor who is often invited to preach outside of my own pulpit. I am invited to speak at schools, conferences, and other special events. But I am most often invited to speak for local churches. I do not take these opportunities lightly. Neither should you, no matter how often you preach as a guest.

A pastor's primary responsibility is to be a faithful steward of the pulpit with which he has been entrusted. He is charged before God to preach the Word (2 Timothy 4:2). And he will answer to God for how faithfully he handles the Word of truth (2 Timothy 2:15). But he is also accountable for what others teach from his pulpit. Therefore, it is a serious matter when a pastor shares his pulpit with another preacher, be it an associate pastor within the church or a guest pastor from outside of it.

I am often asked what to do to get more preaching invitations. I don't know, but I do know how to get invited back. Be a good guest. Here are several helpful hints for being a good guest when you are invited to preach.

BE CLEAR ABOUT THE
PASTOR'S EXPECTATIONS

Why did the pastor invite you? What are his expectations? What are his goals for the meeting? Look for clues in the invitation letter or confirmation email. If necessary, call the pastor to get clarity about what he wants you to do, or not do. Find out the pastor's expectations before you accept the invitation. Respect them as you prepare. And prayerfully follow them when you preach. Simply practice the Golden Rule: Do unto the host pastor as you would have a guest pastor do unto you.

RESPECT THE OCCASION

What is the occasion? Is it a Sunday morning worship service or midweek service? Is it a regular meeting or a special event? Is it evangelistic or discipleship-oriented? Is there an assigned text or theme? Is the event tied to a larger campaign? Is this meeting targeted for a specific group? You should be clear about the nature of the occasion. Then do your best to respect it. If you cannot respect the occasion, it may be best to decline the invitation. You cannot be the host and the guest at the same time. So do not agree to preach at the meeting and then set your own agenda. Speak to the occasion for which you have been invited.

OBSERVE TIME LIMITS

Find out how much time is allotted to you, and consider it a boundary that you must not cross. Ask how much time you should take. Do not accept "Take as much time as you want" as an answer. That's a setup for failure. Ask how long they expect the service to run. Ask what time they expect the service to end. Ask how long the host pastor typically preaches. Keep asking questions until you have clarity about how long you have to speak. Establish the time limits. Then prepare with that time frame in mind. And don't go overtime. Period.

AVOID CONTROVERSIAL SUBJECTS

If a pastor never addresses controversial subjects in his preaching, he is not doing his job. Faithful pastors must tell the truth, the whole truth, and nothing but the truth. But if a guest preacher addresses controversial subjects, he is not doing his job. You are a guest speaker, not the pastor. And some things should only be addressed by the shepherd of the flock, the one who will lead the congregation through difficult terrain. What if the pastor asks you to address some touchy issue? Fine. But still be careful. The authority of the pastor gives him the right to preach certain challenging messages. The fact that he has extended an invitation to you does not transfer that authority to you. The pastor should introduce new, difficult, or controversial subjects to his congregation, not you. Bottom line: don't leave a mess for the pastor to clean up after you leave!

SAY THANK YOU

It is always right to express your thanks to your host for the opportunity to preach. This is not just good pulpit etiquette, it's what your momma taught you. When someone is kind to you, say thanks. Of course, you should thank that pastor privately for the invitation. But it is also appropriate to publicly thank the pastor before the congregation for the opportunity. It is a big thing for a pastor to invite a guest into his pulpit. And it is an even bigger thing that he invited you. He was not obligated to do it, even if you have previously invited him to preach for you. There are many others he could have asked to preach the Word to his people on this occasion.

Acknowledge this fact and express your gratitude for the invitation. In fact, send a note of thanks after the meeting. It is a privilege to be asked to preach. The least you can do is say thank you.

BE YOURSELF

There is great freedom in preaching regularly to the same congregation. A relationship is established. They know what to expect from you, and you know what to expect from them. But preaching to strangers is a different thing entirely. If you are not careful, you can succumb to the pressure to pretend to be something you are not. Just be yourself. Do not pretend to be the pastor, especially if you are an associate filling in for your pastor. If you listen to a man preach each week, it is hard to not pick up some of his pulpit manners and customs. But do not lose yourself in an attempt to be someone else. Do not be a clone. And do not presume authority that is not yours. The congregation knows you are not the pastor. But they will accept you, as long as you do not pretend to be what you are not. The Lord will not hold it against you if you are not someone else. But He will hold it against you if you are not who and what He called you to be.

ASK PERMISSION

Are you not sure about whether you should preach a particular message? Will you preach from a different translation than what the congregation normally uses? Do you plan to use multimedia in the sermon? Will you say something that may be misunderstood? Would you like to make your book or other resources available for sale? Are you considering something out of the norm at that church? Do you plan to extend an invitation or altar call at the end of the sermon? Is something "on your heart" to say or do? Do not press on with it and get the pastor's forgiveness later. Seek his permission first. If in doubt, ask. Get his advice. Make sure the pastor is comfortable with whatever you have planned.

BE CONSERVATIVE

When you are a guest in another pastor's pulpit, it is always best to err on the side of caution. Dress conservatively. It is better to be overdressed than underdressed. But don't be flashy. Don't draw unnecessary attention to yourself. You are there for a worship service, not a fashion show. Don't be a diva. Don't make unreasonable requests. And don't make any demands of your hosts. You are there to serve the congregation, not the other way around. Respect the dignity of the pulpit. Did you get away with that envelope-pushing statement or illustration with your congregation? Good. Leave it there. Strive to be humble, respectful, and sensitive to the environment of the church.

PARTICIPATE IN THE WORSHIP SERVICE

As a guest preacher, the sermon does not start when you stand up to preach. It begins the moment you enter the room. The congregation is looking you over the whole time. They are trying to determine whether they will listen to you before you ever utter one word. Win their goodwill by participating in the worship service. Do not sit in the office or green room until it is time for you to speak. The earlier parts of the service are not your opening act. Come into the service and join the saints in praise to God. Do not sit on the platform reading your manuscript or notes, ignoring what is happening around you. Pay attention. Participate. Be engaged. You want the congregation to continue to worship as you preach. Worship with the congregation before you preach.

BE ON ASSIGNMENT

Pastors must have a long-term perspective. This Sunday matters, and he must give God his best. But next Sunday is coming. And the next. Sunday comes regularly and rapidly. Monday morning turns into Saturday night with blinding speed. Effective pastors must train like marathon runners. But effective guest speakers must train like sprinters. Better yet, consider yourself a special operations soldier. You are dropped into a war zone to carry out a specific assignment. You only have a limited window of opportunity. The helicopter will arrive soon to lift you to safety. You must follow orders and faithfully carry out your preaching mission. Don't view the opportunity as a mere preaching engagement. View it as a divine assignment. Be prepared. Be obedient. Be prayerful. Be faithful. Be diligent. You may never know how that congregation received your message, but strive to hear the Master say, "Well done!"

Chapter 27

BEING AN
ASSOCIATE MINISTER

Going directly from a call to preach to leading a church is extremely rare. And that's a good thing. In fact, going directly from seminary into the pastorate can be just as dangerous—for the new pastor and the potential congregation. You can finish school and think you know it all, only to run full speed into the harsh realities of congregational life that you were not trained to face after all.

Most young preachers need the maturation process that comes from serving with or under another pastor before leading their own congregation. Yet many associate ministers wish they could just skip this process. Pastors sometimes treat associates like their personal flunkies. Congregations sometimes neglect the vital role associate ministers play. Members may view associates as stepparents, substitute teachers, or low-status sidekicks. It can be discouraging to the pastor-to-be. But it doesn't have to be. Your time as an associate minister can be an affirmation of your ministerial call, a time of spiritual development, and a fruitful season of Christian service. Though not every point below relates directly to preaching, the following are ten ways you can maximize your season as an associate minister.

SEEK CLARITY ABOUT YOUR CALLING

Not every associate preacher is called to be a senior pastor. It may be God's will for you to serve alongside another pastor for the duration of your ministry. This is a noble calling. Your ministry is not unimportant because your name is not on the bulletin. Seek the Lord about the calling on your life. Is it missionary work? Should you be in the classroom, rather than the pulpit? Is there an area of specialization—like youth, Christian education, or counseling— the Lord has purposed for you? Or are you called to the pulpit of a local church? Are you supposed to be a lead or senior pastor of a church? Get clarity about your calling and head in that direction.

BE READY TO PREACH AND TEACH

You may not have a scheduled time to preach. Most associates do not. And you may have to share opportunities with other associates, some of whom are more skilled and experienced than you. So take advantage of every chance you get to preach or teach. "Be ready in season and out of season" (2 Timothy 4:2). Don't wait to get a date before you prepare a message. Start getting ready to preach now. Pick a text. Study hard. Write a sermon. Get your pastor's input. Show him by your work that you are ready. And don't wait for Sunday morning spots. Volunteer for a Sunday school class, prayer breakfast, or funeral. Lead a service at a nursing home. Take the lead of a discipleship group. Teach whenever you can. This is the most important thing you can do as an associate minister. Prepare for the pastorate by increasing your skill and experience in ministering the Word.

LEARN EVERYTHING YOU CAN

A senior pastor must still be a perpetual student if he is to maintain an effective ministry. How much more is that the case for associate ministers who hope to become a senior pastor one day! You should view yourself as a student. Consider yourself an intern. Your job is to learn all you can from your pastor and through your home church.

Don't let your pastor have to find you. Show him he can count on you. Be marked present regularly. Get involved. Take the role of a foot-washer. Before you can be a ruler over many things, you must be faithful over a few things. Improve your service. Be willing to participate in behind-the-scenes ministry work, not just "platform" activities. Follow your pastor around. Spend as much time with him as you can. Ask a lot of questions. Listen to the answers. Don't talk too much. Process what you experience. Learn from successes and mistakes. Soak up all the knowledge and wisdom you can get. You never know how God will use your present experiences to prepare you for future opportunities.

BE PROACTIVE ABOUT YOUR GROWTH

It is said that time fixes everything. But that is not true. Time doesn't fix a flat tire. And, by itself, it does not produce a skilled minister. You have to do something to change a flat tire. And you must be intentional about your development as a minister of the gospel. Do not be content to be more pulpit furniture, sitting on the platform without making a contribution. Don't be guilty of ministerial sloth. And don't wait for others to invest in you. Read everything you can get your hands on. Study every opportunity you get. Go to school, if you can. When possible, attend ongoing training events. Seek out your pastor's counsel, guidance, and mentorship.

Ask for assignments that will help you grow. Be willing to lead. Be willing to follow. Don't be indifferent about your ministerial future. Don't wait for something to happen. Don't settle for spiritual mediocrity. Determine to be the best you can be for God.

BE LOYAL TO YOUR PASTOR

Joshua was a better leader than Moses. And Aaron was more spiritual than Moses. But the Lord put the rod in Moses' hand. He was the Lord's appointed leader. He was God's man for that season. Joshua would eventually lead the people of God. But that would not be until the Lord finished the work He had assigned to Moses. Aaron and Miriam got into trouble with the Lord when they usurped Moses' authority. You must respect the one to whom the Lord has given the rod of leadership.

The pastor was voted, called, or selected to lead the church. You were not. It is not your place to run ahead of the pastor or to work against him. You are there to assist him, not fight him. And you should not be a friend to those who would disrespect spiritual leadership in the church. Respect your pastor, even if you are older and wiser. Support him, even if you have been there longer than he has. Honor him, even if you have more training or experience. Pray for him. Help him. Encourage him. Do whatever you can to support him. Be trustworthy. Keep private information confidential. Do not speak against the pastor to members. Do not listen to members speak against the pastor. Beware: what goes around comes around. Treat your pastor the way you will want your members to treat you one day.

HAVE A SERVANT'S SPIRIT

The paradox of Christian discipleship is that the one who would lead must be a servant. The last will be first and the first must be last. The greatest in the kingdom is the one who becomes like a little child. This is the Christian way of leadership. We are servant-leaders. Christian leadership is about submission, not authority. Serving as an associate minister can help you develop a proper attitude toward Christian leadership. Be a servant. Be like Christ. Imitate the one who washed His disciples' feet (John 13). Follow the example of the one who was obedient even to the point of death on a cross. Make yourself available to serve. Serve the Lord with gladness. Serve as unto the Lord, and not men. And don't get offended when you are treated like a servant!

KEEP YOUR EGO IN CHECK

Don't let compliments, encouragements, and opportunities go to your head. You may be a better preacher or leader than your pastor, but it may just be your pride talking. Regardless, there is a reason the Lord has placed you under his leadership, and it is not to compete with the pastor. Be humble. Be submissive. Be faithful. In due time, the Lord will exalt you. Don't exalt yourself!

DO NOT USURP AUTHORITY

If you are not the senior pastor, do not presume authority that is not yours. Do what you are asked to do. Don't take liberties with the opportunities you are given. Don't let leaders or members pressure you to act impetuously. Don't make a golden calf for the people while the leader is away. If in doubt, ask. Or, better yet, don't do it. Stay in your lane.

WAIT YOUR TURN

You have a burden to pastor. It has been your heart's desire for some time. You have done what you can to prepare yourself. But no doors have opened. You are stuck in God's waiting room. Don't get impatient. God knows who you are and where you are. God knows the place He has for you. God also knows how and when to get you there. Don't be weary in well doing. Trust that God's timing is perfect.

LEAVE WHEN IT'S TIME TO LEAVE

You are asking for trouble if you leave an assignment prematurely. God disciplines AWOL soldiers. At the same time, don't stay too long. Don't sit in neutral unnecessarily. Don't hide from your true calling. Don't be a source of confusion or disunity. If you do not respect your leader or cannot follow his leadership, leave. But make sure you leave in a way that doesn't burn bridges.

Chapter 28

WHEN YOU LOSE
YOUR CUTTING EDGE

A friend who is a budding preacher and active associate minister wrote me for advice about what to do when you lose your sense of discipline and devotion. He asked an important question, and it is a real issue. There are times in the ministry when your spiritual vitality is strong. But there can also be times when your devotional life is inconsistent, your sense of communion with God is weak, and your prayer times feel empty. You must not take these times lightly. And you must not be content to let them continue.

The heart is the wellspring of life (Proverbs 4:23). It is also the primary instrument of Christian ministry. Your ministerial work is in vain if it is not done from the overflow of a heart that is devoted to the Lord. You can become anxious and troubled like Martha if you do not sit at the feet of Jesus like Mary (Luke 10:38–42). What should you do when you begin to lose your sense of spiritual devotion and discipline in ministry? Let me respond with a devotional thought from 2 Kings 6:1–7.

The "sons of the prophets"—a group of young preachers—studied under the prophet Elisha. So many lads joined this upstart seminary that they soon ran out of space to house everyone. With Elisha's permission and encouraging presence, the men began to chop down wood near the Jordan River to build a new dormitory.

Imagine the scene. A large group of young men are out in the woods cutting down trees to build a school to train for ministry. Now focus on one young prophet who has borrowed an axe to help with the building project. He is furiously attacking a tree, one mighty blow after another. But after one particularly powerful swing, the handle suddenly goes light in his hands. The force almost knocks him down. He looks up just in time to see his axe head splash into the river. There are a few ripples in the water. Then the river becomes still again. But the young man is a raging sea within. He lost his cutting edge. He lost his power element. He lost the thing that made him effective.

This can happen to any of us. It has surely happened to me at times. There have been seasons when I have been so spiritually dry that I could spit dust. And it can happen to you. (Warning: Don't scoff or judge or dismiss this reality if it hasn't happened to you yet. Thank God. Be humble. And memorize 1 Corinthians 10:12.) What should you do when you lose your cutting edge? Here are five suggestions for making a comeback.

PRACTICE REGULAR SELF-EVALUATION

This young man chopping wood may have lost his cutting edge because of negligence. I'd bet that axe head didn't just fly off the handle all at once. It had been loosening over time. Little by little, it was working itself loose. But he was so busy swinging that he didn't notice. That's how life is. A flat tire is rarely the result of a sudden blowout. There has often been a nail in the tire for some time. So practice regular self-evaluation to ensure your communion with

God is tight. You may not have to recover your axe head if you simply maintain it properly.

TAKE A BREAK

When this young man lost his cutting edge, he stopped swinging. That simple act reflects great wisdom. Think about it. If he would have continued swinging, he would not have been accomplishing anything. He would have only been banging on the wood. He would have only been making noise, wasting time, and losing energy without any progress. So he stopped swinging. So should you. If you sense that you have lost your cutting edge, take a break. Rest. Pray. Reconnect with God. Get back into the Word. Spend time with your family. Clarify your purpose. Return to your first love. For God's sake, please stop swinging! If you have lost your axe head, you are only getting in the way of the real work.

REMEMBER YOU ARE JUST A STEWARD

"Alas, my master! It was borrowed" (2 Kings 6:5). That was the initial response of the budding prophet when he lost his cutting edge. He lamented the loss of the axe head because it did not belong to him. It belonged to someone else. It was borrowed. A kind neighbor permitted him to use his axe. But the axe was not his to keep. It would have to be returned. He would have to answer to the owner for the lost axe head. Likewise, your gifts, talents, position, relationships, and opportunities are not yours. For that matter, you are not your own (1 Corinthians 6:19–20). You are a manager, a steward, a trustee of that which belongs to Another. And you will have to answer to the Lord for all that He has entrusted you to manage.

ASK FOR HELP

The lamentation of the young man was also a cry for help. "Alas, my master!" he said to Elisha. There was nothing he could do about the situation on his own. He needed help. I am not sure he expected Elisha to perform a miracle. But he recognized he needed help. So do you. You cannot recover your cutting edge on your own. Call on the Lord. Ask Him to do for you what you cannot do for yourself. And call on those the Lord has placed in your life for fellowship, encouragement, and accountability. The Enemy wants you to think you are in the battle by yourself. You are not. God has placed people in your life who can help you stay on the right track. Don't be too proud to ask for help.

EXAMINE YOURSELF

Elisha responded to the young man's cry for help with a question: "Where did it fall?" (2 Kings 6:6). This question required the young man to look back, retrace his steps, and think about his situation. Indeed, the unexamined life is rarely effective. Take the time and trouble to examine yourself. Where is your cutting edge? Where did you lose it? When did you lose it? What should you do now? How can you retrieve it?

The story ends with a miracle. Elisha threw a stick into the water, and the axe head began to float. Yes, that's what I said. The iron swam. God sovereignly intervened to restore what was lost. He can do that for you, too, when you find that you've lost your cutting edge.

Chapter 29

DO YOU WANT
TO BE SOMEBODY?

One of my pulpit heroes preached for me at my first church. I had followed his ministry for some time. He was actually mentoring me from afar. But we didn't really know one another. Yet he agreed to preach a meeting for me. I was beyond excited.

I have absolutely no recollection of the service that night. And I could not tell you anything about the sermon he preached if my life depended on it. But I will never forget the conversation afterward in my study.

Food had been prepared for our guests, and a few preachers hung around after the service to eat and chat, including several denominational leaders who had come to hear our special guest. As we sat at the conference table, the denominational leaders began to encourage me to get more involved in the work. Honestly, it felt more like pressure. They dropped the hook with tempting bait. If I would do this and that, it would ensure preaching opportunities and important positions, and other "benefits" would come my way. This was heady stuff for me. As a young pastor, and being new to all of this, it was hard taking it all in.

My guest speaker was not in this conversation. He was not even at the table. But he overheard the discussion and pulled up a chair right next to me. He then began to tell me denominational horror stories he had experienced. The stories were bad. They were filled with corruption and manipulation that didn't match the bait the denominational leaders had offered. And to make matters worse, every time my guest would say the word "convention," he would put extra weight on the first three letters—CONvention.

The denominational leaders' eyes got big. I felt an awkward exchange brewing, if not an outright argument. So I tried to head off an incident by (half) jokingly saying to my guest, "Doc, you know there are denominational leaders at the table with us, don't you?"

"I don't care," was his firm response. He kept talking. I kept listening. But I couldn't make sense of what was going on. Some of the men at the table were his friends. What was he doing? As he kept talking, I recognized that he was not trying to disrespect the other men at the table. He was trying to get my attention. It worked.

He began to list all the conferences and conventions where he had recently spoken. They were places I hoped to speak at one day. Then he asked, "Do you know which one I am a part of?" I already knew the answer. None of them. He kept talking, challenging me to live for God, preach the Word, and serve my congregation. The room eventually emptied out. But he kept talking, assuring me that God would open doors of opportunity for me if I kept my priorities straight.

It was way past midnight, but he was still talking. I didn't say a word. I couldn't. I was too busy crying. He was saying what I desperately needed to hear. More than he could know, these words met me at the right time. I had been too focused on where my "gifts" and "talents" could take me. I was viewing my ministry as a career to build, rather than a calling to fulfill. I was thinking about making my name great, rather than exalting the name of Jesus. I needed to be slapped in the face with a reminder that my only responsibility was to be faithful. The Lord is in charge of personnel placement.

He finally let me up for air. Sort of. After challenging me for several hours, he ended the conversation dismissively. "I hope I have not just wasted my time talking to you," he said. "I hope not. But I think I may have. I think you want to be somebody. I don't want to be somebody. I just want to preach. But I think you want to be somebody."

Through my tears, I finally responded. "I don't want to be somebody, either," I whimpered. "I just want to preach."

That life-changing conversation took place more than two decades ago. But I still wrestle with the temptation to want to "be somebody." I constantly need to remember what I am and what I am not. "But we have this treasure in jars of clay," said Paul, "to show that the surpassing power belongs to God and not to us" (2 Corinthians 4:7).

God uses weak people. The message of the gospel is magnificent. The messengers of the gospel are not. If God is not using you greatly, it has nothing to do with the fact that you are weak. In fact, the problem may be that you are not weak enough. Think about that.

Are you weak enough for God to use you?

Are you weak enough to totally depend on the Lord for strength?

Are you weak enough to stop believing in yourself?

Are you weak enough to lean on others for help?

Are you weak enough to quit using your pain, fear, background, limitations, and circumstances as excuses for not giving God your best?

God uses weak people, not gospel superstars. We are weak and fragile clay pots at the Master's disposal to convey the treasure of the message of Jesus Christ. God uses weak people because He wants everyone to see that the power is His alone (2 Corinthians 12:9). May the Lord continue to help me to be content with the high calling to preach the Word of God and the testimony of Jesus Christ.

What about you? Do you want to be somebody?

Chapter 30

THE BOTTOM LINE
OF CHRISTIAN MINISTRY

In the business world, the bottom line is the last line of a financial statement that shows profit and loss. It reveals whether the company is earning or losing money. And, as they say, the bottom line is the bottom line. This is primarily a business term. But every area of life and labor has a bottom line, crucial factor, or intended outcome. In business, the bottom line is making money, earning profit, and increasing revenue. In education, it is passing tests, making grades, and earning a diploma or degree. In sports, it is winning games, awards, and championships.

Every area has a bottom line. What is the bottom line of Christian ministry? Admittedly, that is a strange question. You would think the answer would be obvious. A ground ball. A no-brainer. Unfortunately, that is not the case. Sadly, many pastors, congregational leaders, and local churches suffer from a ministerial identity crisis, a lack of gospel mission, and misplaced priorities. We do not seem to be clear about what on earth the church of Jesus Christ is to be or do these days. We need to get back to the basics and renew our commitment to the bottom line of Christian ministry.

In 2 Timothy 2:15, Paul says, "Do your best to present yourself to God as one approved, a worker who has no need to be ashamed, rightly handling the word of truth." This is the bottom line of Christian ministry—making sure you please God in everything you do. Ultimately, the only thing that truly matters is whether or not you will be able to end your ministry by hearing the Lord say, "Well done, good and faithful servant" (Matthew 25:21). What does it take to have a life and ministry that is pleasing to God?

PERSONAL EARNESTNESS

Paul instructs, "Do your best to present yourself to God as one approved" (2 Timothy 2:15). Christian ministry deserves your best. You should live and minister with the blood-earnest conviction that if it bears God's name, it deserves your best. The goal is to present yourself to God as one approved. God is the final, ultimate judge of the success or failure of your ministry. He is our target audience. And your ministry will not be rewarded unless you work with all your heart to be a God-pleaser, not a people-pleaser.

Note that Paul did not challenge Timothy to be better than anybody else. He says, "Do your best. . . . " You don't have to compare yourself with others, compete with others, or come in ahead of others. Just give God your best—nothing more, nothing less, nothing else. If you give God your best, it will sustain you when the work is difficult, frustrating, and tiresome. And you will be an approved workman.

The goal of Christian ministry is that you may be approved by God. You know what it means to be approved, don't you? If you use a credit card, ATM card, or debit card, you know what it means to be approved. When they swipe your card, the submitted cost of the item you are trying to buy is either approved or declined. And one day your life and ministry will be swiped through God's sovereign scanning system to determine if you are worthy of a heavenly reward. So live and minister to win God's approval.

MINISTERIAL EXCELLENCE

As Christian workmen, we must be on guard against ministerial sloth. Ministers often fail not because of a lack of giftedness, talent, potential, opportunity, or resources. We fail many times because we are lazy about the things of God. But ministerial excellence takes hard work. Godly living, humble service, wise leadership, unconditional love, steadfast endurance, sound doctrine, and intercessory prayer is hard work. But it is worth what it costs. "For God is not unjust so as to overlook your work and the love that you have shown for his name in serving the saints, as you still do" (Hebrews 6:10). People may forget your work, but God will never forget.

Paul exhorts Timothy to be "a worker who has no need to be ashamed" (2 Timothy 2:15). The concern is about shame before God, not man. It is the God-focused shame of unworthy service. You can be a smashing success with man and a horrible failure with God. You can be a famous minister and yet stand before the Lord and have to introduce yourself (Matthew 7:21–23). The Lord is keeping a record on you. And one day you will have to answer to the Lord for how you have lived your life (2 Corinthians 5:10). No one will have to tell on you. He already knows. There is no hiding place from Him.

So live and minister so that you can be a worker who has no need to be ashamed. Be a workman who has done his work well and can submit it to his superior without hesitation or embarrassment. Live that way. Minister that way. Teach that way. Make it your ultimate goal to hear the Master say, "Well done."

FAITHFUL EXPOSITION

Paul wrote to Timothy, "I charge you in the presence of God and of Christ Jesus, who is to judge the living and the dead, and by his appearing and his kingdom" (2 Timothy 4:1). Stop right there for a moment. What pastoral assignment could be so important that Paul calls on the authority of God, Christ, the final judgment, and the kingdom of heaven to witness as he issues it? Is it church administration? Nope. Is it committee meetings? Nope. Is it pastoral counseling? Nope. Is it hospital visitation? Nope. Is it church growth? Nope. It is none of those things, even though they all have their place. The pastor's primary and central work is stated in the first three words of 2 Timothy 4:2: "preach the word." That imperative is all-important for pastoral ministry.

To carry out this sacred task, you must always be "rightly handling the word of truth" (2 Timothy 2:15). The minister who pleases God must have an unwavering commitment to the faithful exposition of God's Word. God's Word is marked "Handle With Care." You must be careful how you handle the Word of God. The way you handle God's Word determines the way God is going to handle you (Proverbs 30:5–6).

Do not mishandle God's Word. Cut it straight. Proclaim the divine message carefully and correctly. Make it your top priority to study, trust, obey, teach, preach, and defend the Word of truth. And diligently pass it on to the next generation so that it will continue to be faithfully proclaimed and defended after God moves you off the scene (2 Timothy 2:2). If you handle the Word of God rightly, the Lord will be pleased. And the Lord will reward you. Or if I can say it the way I like to say it: If you take care of God's business, God will take care of your business!

So don't mishandle God's Word. Handle it carefully. Handle it correctly. Cut it straight. Don't add to the Word. Fully give yourself to diligently explaining and exhorting the truth of Scripture to the glory of God. Make it your top priority to tell the truth of God!

FROM ONE PASTOR
TO ANOTHER . . .

In *On Pastoring*, H. B. Charles gives 30 instructive reflections on the pastor's heart, leadership, and public ministry, covering topics like:

- Cultivating personal godliness
- Prioritizing your family
- Guarding your ministry effectiveness
- Planning, preparing, and preaching sermons
- Balancing pastoral roles and duties

Being a pastor means wearing many hats, weathering pressure, and bearing great responsibility. Let H. B. Charles be a trusted advisor as you do the serious work of shepherding a flock of God.

ALSO AVAILABLE AS AN EBOOK

It Happens After Prayer

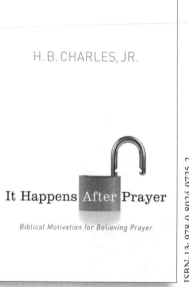

H. B. CHARLES, JR.

It Happens After Prayer

Biblical Motivation for Believing Prayer

ISBN-13: 978-0-8024-0725-2

Whatever the obstacle in your path. Whatever it is that you have tried to move without success. You have not done enough or used all your strength if you have not asked God for help and prayed about it sincerely, diligently, and persistently. In *It Happens After Prayer*, Pastor H. B. Charles, Jr. encourages you to consider your prayer life and know that whatever your need or situation, prayer is the place to begin. You can pray to God with confidence, trusting that He hears and will answer.

Also available as an ebook

MOODY
Publishers™

From the Word to Life

www.MoodyPublishers.com

The Difference Jesus Makes

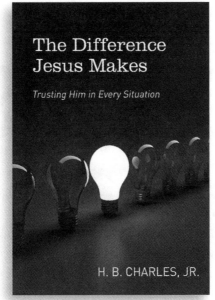

ISBN-13: 978-0-8024-1227-0

Learn the difference Jesus makes as Pastor H. B. Charles, Jr. walks you through Mark 5. This fresh look at active faith, transforming power, and the compassion of Jesus will encourage you to trust Jesus in every situation of life.

Also available as an ebook

MOODY
Publishers™

From the Word to Life
www.MoodyPublishers.com

urbanpraise

Urban Praise, a commercial-free Moody Radio Internet station, offers a soulful blend of rich gospel and urban music. Energize your faith with artists like Kirk Franklin, Israel Houghton, Shirley Caesar, CeCe Winans, Walter Hawkins, and Lecrae, along with bite-size teaching segments from Tony Evans, Crawford Loritts, Melvin Banks, Beth Moore, and others.

www.urbanpraiseradio.org

MOODY Radio™

*From the Word **to Life***